Verbal and Numerical Reasoning Exercises for the Police Recruit Assessment Process

— ASSAULT
— MUG

Verbal and Numerical Reasoning Exercises for the **Police Recruit Assessment Process**

Richard Malthouse
Jodi Roffey-Barentsen

Los Angeles | London | New Delhi
Singapore | Washington DC

Acknowledgements

The authors would like to thank the following for their kind assistance.

Jennifer Clark, Sarah Skultety and Sharon Stratton

First published in 2010 by Learning Matters Ltd
Reprinted 2013

© 2010 Richard Malthouse and Jodi Roffey-Barentsen

British Library Cataloguing in Publication Data

A CIP record for this book is available from the British Library.

All characters, organisations and places mentioned in this publication are fictitious and any resemblance to real persons, living or dead, is purely coincidental.

ISBN: 978 1 84445 462 4

The rights of Richard Malthouse and Jodi Roffey-Barentsen to be identified as the Authors of the Work have been asserted by them in accordance with the Copyright, Design and Patents Act 1988.

Cover design by Topics – The Creative Partnership
Text design by Code 5 Design Associates Ltd
Project Management by Deer Park Productions
Typeset by Kelly Winter
Printed and bound in Great Britain by Ashford Colour Press Ltd., Gosport, Hampshire

Learning Matters
An imprint of SAGE Publications Ltd
1 Oliver's Yard
55 City Road
London EC1Y 1SP

SAGE Publications Inc.
2455 Teller Road
Thousand Oaks, California 91320

SAGE Publications India Pvt Ltd
B 1/I 1 Mohan Cooperative Industrial Area
Mathura Road
New Delhi 110 044

SAGE Publications Asia-Pacific Pte Ltd
3 Church Street
#10–04 Samsung Hub
Singapore 049483

Contents

Introduction

The verbal logical reasoning and numerical reasoning tests, together with an interview, the written exercise and the interactive exercises, make up the police recruit assessment process. Although these tests represent a small part of the overall assessment process, they are important because the results contribute to your overall performance. This book explains exactly what is expected of you in both tests.

Part 1 of this book considers the verbal logical reasoning test. The test is about making sense of the written word, applying logic; not 'verbal' as in spoken. The test is fully described and you are guided through an example. Strategies are discussed which enable you to arrive at the correct answers. The type of thinking associated with this test may be a new experience, as you need to answer each question individually, without making any assumptions. The following chapter offers ten tests which are similar to those in the assessment, to practise your skills.

Part 2 of this book considers the numerical reasoning test. Each element of the test is described and explained in detail, essentially covering the basic principles of numeracy. Throughout Chapter 4 there will be a number of exercises for you to refresh and practise your numeracy skills. As with all skills, the more you practise, the easier it will become. Chapter 5 offers a number of tests which are similar to those in the assessment, to help you to prepare for the test.

Finally, the book discusses the importance of reflective practice, as you need to reflect on your skills and perhaps put some action plans into place. It is strongly recommended that you pace yourself doing the tests, spreading them out over a period of time, addressing any problems that you may encounter.

Examination conditions

You will take both the verbal and numerical reasoning tests with other candidates, therefore the room lay-out may be formal with rows of desks and chairs. According to Cox (2007), you will be informed of the number of questions in the test and the amount of time you have to complete them. Further, you will be given a few practice questions, with the worked-out answers.

On the answer sheet you will find your candidate number, not your name. Do not write on the question paper as this will be used again. If your paper is marked in any way, you can ask for another one. Although a clock will be provided in the room, ensure that you have a watch with you. The use of mobile phones is not allowed during the assessment centre process. There will be no count down, in other words you will be informed only when your time is up. Therefore, it is important that you keep an eye on the time so that you do not get caught out. If you realise you have only a minute left and still have a number of questions to answer, make a very quick 'guestimate': look at the questions very quickly and make an informed estimate. However, if you have just seconds left, ensure that at the very least, you have an answer in each box. In other words: guess. In some assessments, such as medical or aeronautical, an incorrect answer is awarded a negative mark; however, this is not the case with the verbal or numerical reasoning test. Therefore, do not leave any questions unanswered.

When put under pressure, people sometimes do 'silly' things. Firstly, remember the RTQ principle, which stands for Read The Question! On occasion candidates have rushed into answering a question, realising later that the question they answered was different from the actual question. This can lead to panic and frantic changing of answers. Further, be accurate and precise. Sometimes, in their haste to complete the test in time, candidates miss out a question, recording the answers in the wrong place, e.g. question 2 (Q2) was omitted and now the answer to Q3 is placed on the Q2 line, Q4 on the Q3 line and so on. Again, when this mistake is realised, it is usually associated with more frantic activity with a rubber and pencil.

Apart from the time pressures, candidates can be distracted by thinking about:

• the fear of failing the assessment;

• the possibility of the next question being too difficult;

• the questions they have just completed;

• how they did in the previous exercises.

These thoughts are not helpful. You are therefore advised to take care to do what is described as staying in the 'here and now', focusing 100% on the task in hand.

By following the guidelines in this book and practising the questions, there shouldn't be any questions that you cannot answer. Further, it means you will become accustomed to the speed at which you will have to work.

Part 1

The verbal logical reasoning test

Chapter 1

Introduction to the verbal logical reasoning test

OBJECTIVES

By the end of this chapter you will be able to:

• recognise the structure of the verbal logical reasoning test.

Introduction

The verbal logical reasoning test is designed to identify your ability to understand what has been written. You are given a written account and are presented with a number of statements in relation to that account. You have to identify whether the statements are true, false or if it is impossible to say whether they are true or false. This test lasts 25 minutes and there are a total of 31 questions. It takes place under formal examination conditions, which will be discussed at the end of this chapter.

The nature of the verbal logical reasoning test

In essence the verbal logical reasoning test can be seen as a means of testing your ability to find evidence. As stated above, you are given an account and then statements are made in relation to that account. Look at the following example.

> Tom's car is a nine-year-old, red Renault Scenic Mégane. It has an engine capacity of 2 litres and is fuel injected. It has now done just over 100,000 miles but is in generally good condition. It has air conditioning, a CD player and plenty of air bags. It does not have a digital radio or capacity for an MP3 player. Although Tom likes his car, he would prefer a Mercedes.

The text above represents the information you will be given. Next are a number of statements in relation to above account, which will be discussed individually.

1. Tom's car is blue.

You must decide if the answer is:

A – True
B – False
C – Impossible to say

Look back at the account. Tom's car is red and not blue, therefore the answer is B – False.

2. Tom dislikes Hondas.

In the account there is no reference to whether Tom likes or dislikes Hondas. So, there is no evidence to support answer A or B. The answer, therefore, must be C – Impossible to say.

3. Tom has recently had the car MOTed.

Remember, you are looking for evidence. Your previous knowledge and experience may tell you that a car of this age will require an MOT and that it is therefore highly likely that Tom's car has one. Therefore, you may be tempted to select A – True. However that would be an assumption. You have brought something into the thought process, namely your previous knowledge and experience, which will influence your thinking and your subsequent answer. The account does not mention an MOT, therefore there is no evidence to support either A or B. So again the answer is C – Impossible to say.

4. The car does not have the capacity for an MP3 player.

Although the statement is negative in nature, you will look through the account and decide whether what has been said is correct. On this occasion it is correct as it states that there is no capacity for an MP3 player, therefore the answer is A – True.

5. Tom would prefer a BMW.

Reading the account you will realise that the answer is B – False. However, if you were rushing to complete the questions as quickly as possibly you could confuse one car manufacturer with another without thinking. On the other hand you could read too much into the question and consider that if he prefers a Mercedes he would quite likely also prefer a BMW. Beware of making decisions based on your assumptions, which to your brain have now become facts. It is possible to think too hard about something and then rationalise your assumptions. You must deal only with what you have been given.

In short, when approaching the verbal logical reasoning tests it may be useful to put on your metaphorical Sherlock Holmes hat. Approach each question as Sherlock would have done by asking the following: 'Is there evidence to support this statement?' If there is evidence, does it agree with the statement: if it does the answer is A; if it does not agree with the statement, the answer is B; and if there is no evidence the answer is C.

Why are your verbal logical reasoning skills tested? As a police officer you will often be presented with evidence in the form of written accounts. This could be the report of a crime, a statement from a witness, or a transcript of a statement taken under caution. You will be expected to read the statements, reports, accounts etc. and glean from them the salient points, question inconsistencies and note what offences may have been committed and what are referred to as 'the points to prove' (that is, the evidential elements which taken together would be sufficient to prosecute a person). It takes an analytical, logical approach to ensure that this is done professionally. If this process is carried out by someone who did not read the statements properly, jumping to conclusions and assuming things by introducing pseudo facts that were not present, people could be arrested or charged with an offence which they did not commit.

The answer sheet for the test will be provided, and looks like this:

(A)   (B)   (C)

You should select only one for each question, by colouring in the circle that corresponds to your answer. The result of the test is given a grade from A to D.

→ is there evidence 2 support this statement?

→ if there is evidence, does it agree with the statement

Chapter 2

Verbal logical
reasoning practice tests

9.33

This chapter contains ten verbal reasoning tests for you to complete. As already stated, you have 31 questions to answer in 25 minutes. Therefore, you need to keep an eye on the time, to ensure you pace yourself during the test. Although on the day you will be given a separate marking sheet, for the purpose of this book you are asked to place your marks after each part of the test.

The first few tests differ from the assessment centre in that the story line runs through each of the accounts for a full 31 questions. This is intentional and designed to assist your cognitive recall as your brain can make sense of a related narrative or story. This technique is also used to highlight the dangers of assumptions. The information you already have is likely to influence your thinking, but your answer should focus on the account immediately preceding each set of statements.

In the later tests, the accounts have less in common. There are rarely more than six questions in relation to an account, before you are given a different scenario.

Further, as the tests progress, they become much longer and more complicated, in order to incrementally improve your ability to complete the tests. By the time you finish these tests, the assessment centre verbal logical reasoning tests will seem very straightforward. The purpose of this book is not to give you a long list of tests, but to prepare you adequately for the tests; the two things are very different.

VERBAL LOGICAL REASONING PRACTICE TEST 1

Kiri Nunn was crossing the High Street at 13.45 when she was hit by a car which then sped off at high speed. The only known facts are that:

- Kiri has worked as a reporter for the *Eastshire Times* for the last five years;

- she was due to meet a local informant regarding a big story;

- drugs dealing is on the increase in Eastshire;

- she has made some enemies during her career;

- she was willing to pay for the story;

- the speed on the stretch of road where she was hit is restricted to 40mph.

A – True

B – False

C – Impossible to say

1.	Kiri was intentionally run over by drug dealers.	A	B	**C**
2.	Kiri has no enemies.	A	**B**	C
3.	The car sped off at speeds over 40mph.	A	B	**C**
4.	Three years ago Kiri worked as a reporter.	A	**B**	C
5.	She was going after a big drugs story.	A	B	**C**

The emergency services were called. The only facts known are that:

- the police arrived at 14.21 and the ambulance arrived at 14.23;

- Kiri was suspected of having a broken pelvis and head injuries;

- at that time two witnesses made themselves available to the police;

- one witness stated the car was a black Jaguar, the other thought is was a dark blue Aston Martin;

- one witness saw a large dent in the bonnet of the car which hit Kiri;

- there is CCTV covering the location of the collision.

A – True

B – False

C – Impossible to say

Base your answers only on the account immediately above.

---

6. The ambulance arrived before the police.   A   B   C

7. There were more than two witnesses.   A   B   C

8. The car was dark in colour.   A   B   C

9. The impact caused a dent in the car which hit Kiri.   A   B   C

10. Two witnesses made themselves available later that day.   A   B   C

Kiri was conveyed to the Eastshire hospital by ambulance. The only facts known are that:

- the ambulance arrived at the hospital at 15.49;

- Kiri was conscious upon arrival at the hospital;

- she was seen by medical staff immediately;

- her mobile phone rang and showed that the caller's number was withheld;

- police called the ICE number on Kiri's phone, contacting her partner;

- Kiri was wearing a neck brace in case of neck or spinal injuries.

A – True

B – False

C – Impossible to say

Base your answers only on the account immediately above.

---

11. Kiri was suffering a spinal injury.   A   B   C

12. The local informant tried to call Kiri on her mobile phone.   A   B   C

13. Kiri's partner was a man.   A   B   C

14. Kiri was unconscious on arrival at hospital.   A   B   C

15. The ambulance arrived at the hospital at 15.49.   A   B   C

At the time of the collision involving Kiri the informant had seen everything from a nearby bus stop. The only facts that are known are that the informant:

- recognised the driver as being a drug dealer;

- was frightened;

- called the *Eastshire Times* from their mobile phone anonymously and explained what had happened;

- did not speak to the police at the scene;

- called Kiri on their mobile;

- was an aspiring drug dealer who wanted control of the drug dealing in that area.

A – True

B – False

C – Impossible to say

Remember, do not assume! Base your answers . . .

---

16. The informant was male.   A   B   C

17. The informant had the telephone number of the *Eastshire Times*.   A   B   C

18. The informant spoke to the police at the scene.   A   B   C

19. The informant was a compulsive liar.   A   B   C

20. The informant was relaxed.   A   B   C

Back at the hospital Kiri has been x-rayed and her injuries treated. She has made a statement to police. The only facts that are known are that:

- Kiri will stay in hospital for at least four weeks depending on any complications;

- Kiri described the driver of the car that ran her over as being male, 25 to 34, black hair, dark skin, wearing a dark brown hoodie;

- the police found a front number plate at the scene relating to a dark blue Jaguar XK8 4.2 litre convertible;

- their investigations reveal that the car is registered to a well-known drugs dealer;

- two suspicious looking men have been spotted on the hospital CCTV hanging around the ward in which Kiri is situated;

- The police, who are still present, have been informed.

A – True

B – False

C – Impossible to say

Remember . . .

---

21. The driver that hit Kiri was Asian.	A	B	~~C~~
22. The car had been used in drugs crime previously.	A	B	~~C~~
23. Two drug dealers are on the hospital grounds.	A	B	C
24. Kiri will be able to leave hospital after three weeks.	A	B	C
25. Police found a number plate relating to a Jaguar XK8 4.2 litre convertible.	A	B	C
26. The hospital benefits from CCTV.	A	B	C

Following the call in relation to the men spotted on CCTV, police made two arrests. The only facts that are known are that:

- the arrested men were known associates of a notorious drugs dealer;
- when the house of one of the men was searched by police, the Jaguar involved in the accident was found in his garage;
- when questioned the men stated that they were looking for a poorly relative;
- police investigations revealed that no relatives of the men were being treated at the hospital;
- CCTV shows the men talking on their mobile phones;
- upon arrest the men were found to be half brothers.

A – True

B – False

C – Impossible to say

Remember . . .

---

27. The arrested men are drug dealers.	A	B	C
28. One of the arrested men was the driver of the Jaguar.	A	B	C
29. The men had a poorly friend at the hospital.	A	B	C
30. The men were carrying weapons.	A	B	C
31. The men are related to each other.	A	B	C

VERBAL LOGICAL REASONING PRACTICE TEST 2

12:36

The parking in the Eastshire Shopping Centre is causing problems for some disabled and elderly people. The only facts that are known are that :

- owing to essential resurfacing work, 200 parking spaces have been lost;
- these include 50% of those dedicated to disabled drivers;
- the shopping centre car park is open 06.00–22.00 and is one minute away from the shops;
- only 120 spaces remain in total with just ten for disabled users and ten for guardians with children present;
- Ruth and John were unable to find a suitable space and were forced to drive round for nearly an hour before they found one;
- at its worst, the line of traffic was nearly up to Central Parade.

---

1. The total number of disabled parking spaces, prior to the maintenance, was 20.   A   B   C

2. The car park is open for a total of 18 hours.   A   B   C

3. If guardians wish to park in the allocated bays for guardians with children, their children must be present.   A   B   C

4. Ruth and John have disabilities.   A   B   C

5. Central Parade is over 600 metres from the car park.   A   B   C

Ruth and John were later involved in a problem with an escalator within the Eastshire Shopping Centre. The only facts that are known are that:

- a youth, running up the escalator, bumped into Ruth and knocked her over;
- John managed to catch Ruth but lost his balance;
- they both fell, landing on the steps of the escalator;
- the security guards were called to investigate;
- as Ruth and John were unhurt, they were taken to the security office and a full report was made;
- returning to his car, John realised that his car keys were missing.

6. The youth bumped into John.   A B C

7. Ruth lost her balance.   A B C

8. They both hurt themselves on the escalator.   A B C

9. John lost his car keys as he fell.   A B C

10. A full report was made at the scene of the incident.   A B C

Ruth and John take a taxi home and realise they have no way of letting themselves into their house. The only facts that are known are that:

- at 15.55 hrs Ruth tries to get into the garage where the spare key is kept hidden in an old paint pot;

- John locked the garage before going out today so Ruth goes to the next-door neighbour, Mrs Tait, to phone for a locksmith, but she doesn't tell John about her intention;

- at 15.57 hrs John decides to break into the house and so he smashes a small window leading into the kitchen with a brick that has been left by the back door for years;

- at 15.58 hrs a neighbour (on the opposite side to where Ruth has gone) overhears and, not seeing their car on the drive, dials 999 and requests the police;

- at 15.59 hrs John opens another, larger window and squeezes in and opens the back door. As he does so he notices the garage key lying under where the brick had been;

- at that moment the police, who were nearby, arrive to see him surrounded by broken glass and holding a brick. They are very interested in his explanation and consider detaining him but decide against it.

---

11. The spare key is in an old flower pot in the garage.   A B C

12. John locked the garage.   A B C

13. The police arrive at 15.59.   A B C

14. The key that was under the brick is the key for the back door.   A B C

15. John was detained for questioning.   A B C

The situation is resolved without John being arrested. John offers Ruth, Mrs Tait and the two police officers a coffee. The only facts that are known are that:

- Stuart, one of the police officers, has coffee with skimmed milk and no sugar as he is dieting. He would like a biscuit, his favourite is a digestive, but will decline if offered;

- Kim, the other police officer, prefers her coffee with full-fat milk, two sugars and as many biscuits as are offered;

- Ruth has her coffee black with a sweetener but does not eat biscuits;

- Mrs Tait has tea with semi-skimmed milk and no sugar. Her preferred biscuits are milk chocolate with a layer of caramel;

- John does not care how his coffee looks and will have it black or white, with or without sugar, provided it is accompanied by a custard cream or two. Today he has it white without sugar. *it is a buiscuit !!*

16. Kim, Stuart, Mrs Tait and John like biscuits.   A   B   **C**

17. John would prefer a cup of tea.   A   B   C

18. John would like a biscuit but is dieting.   A   B   C

19. Ruth and Mrs Tait have no sugar.   A   B   C

20. Kim, Mrs Tait, Ruth, Stuart and John all partake of a
    cup of coffee.   A   B   C

The window is replaced and the other car key is found. Ruth and John go out for the day to the seaside with their grandchildren Megan, aged three, James, aged five, and Amelia, aged eight. The only facts that are known are that:

- at the seaside Amelia asks for an ice cream and John agrees. The ice-cream van is within sight so the children are allowed to go together, provided they stay together. John and Ruth remain on the beach;

- on the way James and Amelia see a toilet and decide they can't wait;

- Megan being left outside makes her way to the ice-cream van. Just as she gets close it moves away a little down the seafront. She follows and, just as she gets near, it again moves a little further down the seafront;

- this continues until Megan and the van are out of sight;

- James and Amelia emerge from the facilities and, not seeing Megan, go back to their grandparents, where they assume Megan has gone, because there is no sight of the ice-cream van.

15

21. James asked for an ice cream and John agreed.   A   B   C

22. The children are allowed to get ice cream provided they stay away from danger.   B   A   B   C

23. Amelia and James assume that Megan has gone back to the beach.   A   B   C

24. Every time the ice-cream driver sees Megan approach he moves on down the road.   A   B   C

25. Megan is in danger.   A   B   C

Amelia and James return to the beach. The only facts that are known are that:

- they see John on the beach as Ruth is in the sea swimming. James and Amelia assume that Megan is in the sea with Ruth;

- Ruth finishes her swim and returns. Then Amelia asks where Megan is and Ruth asks the same of her;

- an element of mild panic is felt by Ruth and James;

- John hears the ice-cream van in the distance and has an idea;

- Ruth, Amelia and James go back to the facilities. Amelia is crying;

- John goes in the direction of the ice-cream van, feeling sick inside. He calls the police as he walks;

- John finds Megan sitting in the ice-cream van next to the driver; she is eating and wearing an ice-cream. 'Are you the father?' asks the ice-cream van driver. 'I called the police – she must have walked half a mile.'

26. It was assumed by John that Megan was in the sea with Ruth.   A   B   C

27. Ruth and Amelia both asked where Megan was.   A   B   C

28. Ruth and Amelia felt slightly panicked.   A   B   C

29. Both John and the ice-cream man called the police.   A   B   C

30. Megan was frightened.   A   B   C

31. Megan ate strawberry ice-cream.   A   B   C

VERBAL LOGICAL REASONING PRACTICE TEST 3

IS

Eastshire residents are not happy with the local council's proposals to introduce a number of new initiatives. This includes the introduction of the congestion charge. The only facts that are known are that:

- the congestion charge zone will follow the boundaries of the Parish of St John's and will extend up to, but not including, the A334 ring road;

- it will be in force between the hours of 8 a.m. and 6 p.m. Monday to Saturday. It will not apply to Sundays or bank holidays;

- the cost of entering the zone will be £10 per day; those who enter the zone without a valid ticket will be charged £25 retrospectively. A fine of £50 is payable for those not making a retrospective payment within 14 days of entering the congestion zone;

- the only exceptions will be motorcycles, taxis, disabled drivers and electronically powered vehicles;

- those who live within the congestion zone will not be subject to a charge;

- the congestion zone will be piloted between 3 May and 22 November.

---

1. The A334 is exempt from the congestion charge.   A   B   C

2. According to the local council, drivers of cars with an engine capacity below 800cc are exempt from the charge.   A   B   C   ←

3. Vehicles belonging to the residents living inside the congestion zone are permitted to drive within the zone on a bank holiday.   A   B   C

4. The pilot will last no longer than 5 months.   A   B   C

5. If you make a mistake and drive into the zone without a valid ticket and pay within a period of 24 hours the fee will be £12.   A   B   C

A further proposed change is that of creating a pedestrian zone in the town centre. The only facts that are known are that:

- the pedestrian zone will encompass the roads adjacent to the Eastshire Shopping Centre to create a safe oasis for shoppers;

- all parking in the streets abutting the Shopping Centre is to be suspended;

- no loading or unloading is permitted by any vehicle; there are no exceptions. Vehicles which require unloading for local shops in the area should be within the Eastshire Shopping Centre. The goods to be conveyed from there to the specific premises should be moved using the electronic trolleys located within the Centre;

- any vehicle found parked within the area will be removed by the local authority contractors who are exempt from the scheme. A fine of £50 will be levied on any such vehicle;

- the council proposes to enclose the area with suitable bollards when sufficient funds are found;

- this scheme will be introduced with immediate effect.

6.	The aim of the zone is to reduce the rate of accidents.	A	B	C
7.	Electronic cars are exempt and can enter the zone.	A	B	C
8.	A fine of £50 will be charged for any person entering the pedestrian zone.	A	B	C
9.	Where vehicles are delivering to local shops arrangements should be made with the local council, which will issue permits.	A	B	C
10.	Eventually bollards will be introduced along with a seating area and various plants.	A	B	C

Further to the restriction on vehicular traffic the council further proposes a curb on the wearing of clothing referred to as 'hoodies' within the aforementioned pedestrian zone. The only facts that are known are that:

- recently youths wearing hoodies have been found to be responsible for a significant number of antisocial type crimes;

- these include general annoying behaviour such as congregating outside the Eastshire Centre on the benches, drinking to excess, swearing and spitting;

- the wearing of hoodies makes it difficult for the authorities to identify the individuals using CCTV alone, as they are able to cover their faces with ease;

- it is believed that some youths are selling drugs; again these people are covering their faces when entering the area, making the use of CCTV pointless;

- on occasion fighting has broken out between various gangs of youths; again the problem of identification is exacerbated by the use of hoodies;

- the ban will take place from the first of next month and will be enforced by the police and the local council. Any person found wearing a hoodie will be removed on the first occasion, fined on the second and may face a permanent ban if subsequently found to be ignoring the ban.

---

11. Youths wearing hoodies have been responsible for antisocial crimes.

      A   B   C

12. The main problem is that of identification, exacerbated by the youths wearing a combination of hoodies and sunglasses.

      A   B   C

13. The ban came into force on the 1st of last month and is set to deal with the problem.

      A   B   C

14. The ban will be enforced by the police and local authority as sufficient funding has been granted by the government.

      A   B   C

15. Anyone found wearing a hoodie will be removed form the pedestrian area if found ignoring the ban on a second occasion.

      A   B   C

As part of the Modernising Eastshire project the council proposes a scheme designed to socialise the elderly. The only facts that are known are that:

- all members of the community who are 70 years and over are invited to attend the Eastshire community centre between 10 a.m. and 2 p.m. on Mondays, Wednesdays and Fridays;

- the cost to the individuals will be £1 per visit, to go towards the cost of refreshments;

- a light lunch is served between 12 noon and 1 p.m.;

- vegetarian, halal, kosher and other specific dietary requirements will be catered for where specifically requested;

- a bus will be available to collect attendees from 24 locations in and around the Eastshire area. There is no cost for this service for those 70 and over;

- entertainment will be provided and the council welcome any suggestion for appropriate activities.

---

16. All attendees who wish to attend must be retired.

      A   B   C

17. A fee of £12 per month is levied for refreshments.

      A   B   C

18. Lunch is provided between 12 noon and 1 p.m. on all weekdays.

      A   B   C

19. The bus service is free to those over 70 and a fee of £3
    is charged to all other travellers.   A   B   C

20. Eastshire council welcome any suggestions for
    appropriate menus.   A   B   C

The Modernising Eastshire project includes a scheme designed to assist parents by improving childminding facilities. The only facts that are known are that:

- the Hayway playground and childminding facilities (located at the rear of the Eastshire Shopping Centre) will be utilised for this purpose;

- parents and carers will be able to leave their children at the facilities while they shop. They can take advantage of the scheme between the hours of 8 a.m. and 8 p.m. Monday to Saturday;

- the aim of the project, according to David Ward, Cultural and Community Development Manager, is to alleviate the stress of bringing up small children;

- parents and carers with children between the ages of two to five inclusive will be eligible to attend this scheme. The children will be permitted to stay without charge for a total of two hours. After this time a fee of £10 per half hour will be levied for the first hour and then £15 for each subsequent half hour;

- if any child is left for over 4 hours without their parents or carer contacting the facilities, the manager, Ms Duff, will inform the local social services as they will be assumed to have been abandoned;

- Sam Denton, a local resident whose children are all aged between two and five, is reported as being delighted with the scheme as she has been using a similar scheme at the Hayway playground but has had to pay £1 per child per hour for the facility;

- she has five children and used the facility twice a week for two hours on each occasion.

---

21. Only parents will be permitted to use the facilities.   A   B   C

22. David Ward has long been promoting such schemes
    within the council.   A   B   C

23. If a child is left for two and a half hours, the parent or
    carer will face a charge of £35.   A   B   C

24. If a parent or carer informs the Hayway that they will
    be late by over four hours social services will be informed
    by Ms Duff, who will assume that the child has been
    abandoned.   A   B   C

25. Sam Denton will save at least £20 per week with the introduction of this scheme.

A   B   C

26. Sam Denton is delighted with David Ward.

A   B   C

The Modernising Eastshire project includes another scheme designed to prevent dogs from fouling the footpaths within the pedestrian zone outside the Eastshire Shopping Centre. The only facts that are known are that:

- there is a significant problem with dogs fouling the pavements and grass areas outside the Eastshire Shopping Centre;

- it is proposed that dedicated bins and bags should be provided in the area for dog owners to dispose of the excrement;

- bye laws are already in place prohibiting dogs fouling the area. The council concludes that the bye laws are not being adequately enforced;

- the police and local authority will be on hand to patrol the area and will pay particular attention to any breach of the bye laws;

- the council will work in partnership with the *Eastshire Times* newspaper to promote the scheme and inform local residents;

- the scheme will be introduced at the end of this month and it is estimated that the council will save a considerable amount of money by not employing people whose job it is to clean the area.

---

27. There is a minor problem with dogs fouling the pavements and grass areas outside the Eastshire Shopping Centre.

A   B   C

28. At present the local bye laws are enforced adequately by the police and local authority.

A   B   C

29. Local residents will be made aware of the scheme via the *Eastshire Times* newspaper.

A   B   C

30. The scheme has been introduced for a month.

A   B   C

31. The council anticipates making savings of over £1,500 in the first year alone.

A   B   C

VERBAL LOGICAL REASONING
PRACTICE TEST 4

11.49

An armed robbery occurred in the jewellers in the Eastshire Shopping Centre. The only facts that are known are that:

- five masked people were involved in the robbery; three were riding motorcycles and two were carried pillion. The pillion passengers entered the jewellers;

- two wore crash helmets with scarves around their faces. Two passers-by thought that one was wearing a pig mask underneath the helmet;

- they wore mostly black clothing, with gloves and very large coats;

- the motorcycles were all Yamahas and were over 600cc. Two of them were dark blue in colour, the other mostly black;

- as they approached they made a lot of noise by revving their engines and were seen to drive dangerously quickly within the Eastshire Centre itself;

- the jewellers is adjacent to the main entrance of the Eastshire Shopping Centre.

---

1. Five of the robbers were on motorcycles and three of them entered the jewellers.   A   ~~B~~   C

2. All the robbers wore crash helmets which were black.   A   B   C

3. All the motorcycles were over 600cc.   ~~A~~ ~~B~~ C

4. One passer-by thought that two of the robbers were wearing pig masks.   A   B   C

5. All the motorcycles were made by the same manufacturer.   ~~A~~ B   C

A witness to the robbery reported a clear and unobstructed view to the incident. The only facts that are known are that:

- the passer-by was across the other side of the corridor near the entrance to the Eastshire Shopping Centre and they saw the motorcycles approach;

- the passer-by estimated that they were standing about one bus length away from the jewellers; they could see what was happening quite clearly as there were no obstacles of any kind between themselves and the robbers;

- they state that the robbery took place at about 09.30 and was over in no time at all, probably under two minutes it seemed;

- they remember one of the motorcycles in particular as it looked as if it had been scratched quite badly on the left-hand side. This motorcycle was dark blue in colour. The witness also noticed that one of the motorcyclists was wearing a distinctive boot which featured Velcro on the side and a red letter V with what appeared to have a ring like the planet Saturn around it.

6. The passer-by heard the motorcycles before seeing them.   A   B   C

7. The distance from the passer-by to the motorcycles was about a bus length away.   A   B   C

8. It seemed to the passer-by that the robbery was over in under two minutes.   A   B   C

9. One of the motorcycles had been involved in an accident as it was scratched along one side.   A   B   C

10. The boot of one of the motorcyclists had a distinctive marking in the shape of a V and the ring of Uranus around it.   A   B   C

The owner of the jewellery shop, Mrs Harwood, explained what happened inside the shop. The only facts that are known are that:

- she heard a very loud noise coming from outside that sounded like revving and skidding;

- the next thing she knew, two men had burst into the shop and were shouting at her. At that time they pointed their guns at her and she was very frightened;

- the robbers shouted at her to get down and she was surprised to hear a woman's voice. She got down on the floor and hid her face in her hands as the robbers had started smashing glass to get to the jewellery;

- she lay for what seemed ages and dared not move. She didn't hear them say anything further but she couldn't hear much because she was so frightened;

- she heard the motorcycles move away from the Centre but stayed where she was as she was in shock;

- someone came in and found her on the floor, they helped her up and carefully took the glass out of her hair and clothes. Very soon after that the police arrived, but it was too late as the robbers had all gone.

11. Mrs Harwood saw two armed robbers come into the shop.   A   B   C

12. She saw what she thought were big guns pointing at her by the robbers.   A   B   C

13. She hid her face in her hands because the robbers were smashing the glass to get to the jewellery. A B C

14. Someone found her on the floor, called the police and helped her get the glass out of her hair. A B C

15. The robbers were probably a professional group. A B C

Detective Inspector Andrews was leading the subsequent investigation. The only facts that are known are that:

- the group is suspected of committing four other robberies in and around the county;

- they are very quick and appear to know where to find the most valuable jewellery;

- seven individuals are known to be involved in the actual robberies;

- they are willing to use force if confronted and have shot one shop owner in the legs;

- motorcycles are used on every occasion and CCTV has identified that they travelled due south following the robbery;

- at some stage they disappear completely from other cameras or recording devices.

---

16. The group committed four other robberies in and around the county. A B C

17. More than six members are known to be involved with the robberies. A B C

18. In previous robberies firearms have been used on more than one occasion. A B C

19. Following the robbery at the Eastshire Centre they followed the direction that took them south. A B C

20. At some point in the robbers' journey they disappear from recording devices. A B C

A member of the public who is willing to provide intelligence has offered a number of details. The only facts that are known are that:

- the robbers are between 19 and 24 years of age;

- on every occasion the same two robbers, a male and female, pose as an engaged couple looking for a ring. During this time they engage in formal reconnaissance, noting the location of the most valuable goods;

- the jewels are transported to the continent via the ferries as the robbers believe the chances of being stopped for terrorist activity is far greater than for handling stolen goods;

- those transporting the jewels do not come into direct contact with the firearms. They believe that this will prevent forensic transfer;

- the gang use motorcycles but change the registration numbers to match those used by other bikes in the area;

- at some stage during the getaway the motorcycles drive into a large lorry, which is waiting at a suitable location, out of sight of the members of public and any helicopters. Here they change clothes, package the jewellery and make off on legal motorcycles.

21. The robbers are well organised and are careful to ensure the only jewellers they hit are easily accessible to motorcycles.   A   B   C

22. The same two robbers pretend to be newly engaged.   A   B   C

23. Ferries are used to export the jewels as the robbers believe the police will not suspect them of using this method.   A   B   C

24. The robbers believe they are forensically aware.   A   B   C

25. The registration numbers on the motorcycles are chosen especially to match vehicles in the area in which the robbery will take place.   A   B   C

26. A small lorry is used to assist the robbers' get away.   A   B   C

Detective Inspector Andrew's investigation is progressing well. The only facts that are known are that:

- the boot identified by the passer-by at the time of the robbery is a Vega Matrix Leather Motorcycle Boot. This features the red letter V and the Saturn-like ring around the V;

- during one robbery it was noticed that on a glove of one of the robbers, the trigger finger had been cut away to aid shooting. A finger print was later found in blood where the glass had cut someone during the robbery;

- various CCTVs had captured the features of the two robbers as they were employed on reconnaissance activities;

- a member of the public reported seeing the motorcycles enter a large lorry in the countryside shortly after the Eastshire robbery;

- forensic evidence established a suspect. Intelligence confirmed the identity of one robber;
- as a result three of the robbers in the Eastshire robbery were arrested at 5 a.m. this morning.

---

27. The finger print of a robber was found during one robbery.   A   B   C

28. The finger print was found in the robber's blood.   A   B   C

29. A Vega Matrix boot features a red letter V.   A   B   C

30. The lorry was seen entering the countryside by a member of public.   A   B   C

31. All robbers responsible for the Eastshire robbery were arrested at 5 a.m.   A   B   C

VERBAL LOGICAL REASONING PRACTICE TEST 5

The football season is about to begin again and the Eastshire football club are making the necessary preparations with the police and local council. The only facts that are known are that:

- the parking situation is causing problems for residents in the areas close to the football club. When questioned the fans stated that they experienced no problems parking;

- at about 30 minutes before the start of a game large numbers of fans crossing the road to enter the football club are causing problems for the free flow of traffic in that area;

- Eastshire football team will be relegated if they fail to achieve the necessary points this season;

- rival fans from Northshire have suggested that, because of their defeat last season, trouble may occur;

- the local police have suggested that there are no extra police officers available to assist with the anticipated problems this season. They will, however, conduct talks with the stewards to discuss their needs;

- the police have suggested that the club should consider what it can do to assist with the traffic congestion, the anticipated trouble and the fans crossing the road both before and after a match.

---

1. Parking in the areas close to the football club is causing problems for fans.   A   B   C

2. At about 30 minutes before a match free flow of traffic is being affected by rival gangs crossing the road to enter the football club.   A   B   C

3. Northshire will be relegated if they fail to achieve the necessary points this season.   A   B   C

4. The police have requested more funding from the government to police football matches etc.   A   B   C

5. The police will assist the club by training the stewards to cover some activities traditionally undertaken by the police.   A   B   C

The Eastshire cricket team have relocated and have found a suitable plot; however, a number of difficulties have become apparent. The only facts that are known are that:

- owing to the insistence of some of the more influential members of the club, the purchase of the premises and grounds were rather rushed. As a consequence the club faces some difficulties;

- the proposed site does not benefit from adequate parking facilities. Whereas the present parking accommodates 300 parking spaces, the proposed site will have fewer than 150 spaces;

- one side of the proposed cricket ground borders a main road. The fence in place at present is insufficient to guarantee the safety of passing vehicles. This is due to the height of the fence;

- the new location benefits from a brand-new club house; however, it was not purpose-built and as such is relatively insecure, not benefiting from shutters nor any means of preventing acts of vandalism whilst the building is empty;

- unfortunately, a tree that sits more or less in the centre of the cricket field has found to be the subject of a Tree Preservation Order (TPO) and cannot be removed. The cedar tree is old and large;

- law on TPOs is in Part VIII of the Town and Country Planning Act 1990 ('the Act') and in the Town and Country Planning (Trees) Regulations 1999.

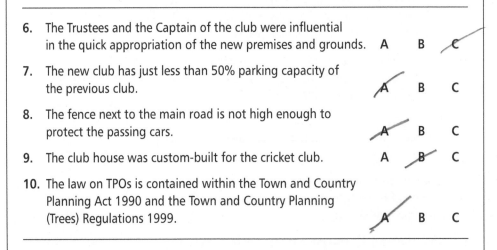

6. The Trustees and the Captain of the club were influential in the quick appropriation of the new premises and grounds.   A   B   C

7. The new club has just less than 50% parking capacity of the previous club.   A   B   C

8. The fence next to the main road is not high enough to protect the passing cars.   A   B   C

9. The club house was custom-built for the cricket club.   A   B   C

10. The law on TPOs is contained within the Town and Country Planning Act 1990 and the Town and Country Planning (Trees) Regulations 1999.   A   B   C

There is trouble at the Eastshire Tennis club. One of the members has been found guilty of highly inappropriate behaviour. The only facts that are known are that:

- the committee has gathered together to consider what action they are entitled to take in accordance with the Eastshire Tennis Club Constitution as the behaviour of the member is very serious;

- the committee may expel any member who offends against the rules of the club or whose conduct, in the opinion of two thirds of the committee, renders him or her unfit for membership;

- before any member can be expelled from the club the Secretary must give him or her 14 days written notice to attend a meeting in the presence of the committee;

- the individual must be informed of the nature of the complaint made against him or her;

- no member may be expelled unless he or she is first given an opportunity of appearing before the committee and answering the complaints made against him or her;

- in the event of expulsion the member will forgo all monies paid within the current term of membership.

Rinunciare a

(Based on the Harlow Tennis Club *Constitution* (2009))

11. The committee's action is restricted to the rules within the constitution.　　　　　　　　　　　　　　A　B　C

12. The committee may expel any member provided the individual has offended against the rules and provided two thirds of the committee are in agreement.　　　　A　B　C

13. Before a member can be expelled they must be invited to attend the meeting. This can be done by phone or email.　A　B　C

14. The individual must be informed of the nature of the complaint made against them; this must be done in the presence of the committee.　　　　　　　　　A　B　C

15. In the event of expulsion the member will be paid back all the money paid within the current term of membership.　A　B　C

The Eastshire Boomerang Club is celebrating its ten year anniversary this year; it is proposed that various activities should take place to celebrate. The only facts that are known are that:

- James Reed, the club founder, is keen to ensure that the events include the members' families both old and young. James has been a keen boomerang thrower for nearly 30 years now;

- a BBQ has been proposed with a vegetarian option and the event will be alcohol free;

- the cost of the celebrations mean that each adult will pay £7.50, children and OAPs £5; a family ticket will cost £20 for two adults and two children, plus £5 per additional child;

- the venue will be held at the New Eastshire Cricket ground. The only foreseeable problems are limited parking and the presence of a large tree in the middle of the field.

- the celebrations will begin at 2 p.m. with a display of various boomerang techniques, followed by speeches and awards to deserving members of the club;

- Fridolin Frost (Frido) will be available to sign autographs and chat with members during the event.

---

16. James has been a keen boomerang player for ten years now.   A   B   C

17. James once threw in competition against Fridolin Frost.   A   B   C

18. The event will attract over 150 families.   A   B   C

19. The cost of the event for a family of six (two adults and four children) will be £30.   A   B   C

20. Fridolin Frost will be awarding the prizes.   A   B   C

The Eastshire Rugby Club has been in the *Eastshire Times* again. A recent report by Holly Bright makes interesting reading. The only facts that are known are that:

- Stuart (Whacker) Wilkinson and Andy (Windy) Windatt are both fit and ready for this year's season. Andy was quoted as saying, 'I got my weight down from 20 to 18 stone and feel much better for it.'

- Stuart has been nursing a recurring injury to his neck but is confident that it is fully healed. The bones in his neck have been fused so he finds neck movement difficult but as he said, 'I go so fast why look behind?'

- Jacqui Mallet-Smith, the ~~team medic,~~ said of the team, 'They work hard and play hard, you should expect a few bumps and scrapes, especially in the scrum. I think there is a 50/50 chance of us holding the cup this year which is an improvement on last year.'

- Bob Jeffery, the team physiotherapist, said, 'It's brilliant, the players have really given their all to get their fitness up and their medical problems have all but disappeared, I think they will do brilliantly again this year; it's all thanks to Jacqui. I'm particularly looking forward to the introduction of the women's teams,' he added with a smile;

- according to the *Eastshire Times* the star players are back on form and they have new blood in the team in the shape of Urkovskis, Veispeks-Veisbachs, Zacharovskis and Sturstep-Sturit;

- the Chairman Steve Hill said, 'It's a great place to work here, everyone is so welcoming. I used to work for the Northshire lot; they couldn't run from one end of the pitch to the other without stopping to check their hair in a mirror. This year the cup is ours!'

21. Andy Windatt has lost weight.	A	B	C
22. Stuart Wilkinson plays in the wing at number 13.	A	B	C
23. Jacqui Mallet-Smith feels that the chances of winning are better than last year.	A	B	C
24. Recently there has been an influx of Eastern Europeans to Eastshire.	A	B	C
25. Bob Jeffery is looking forward to the introduction of the women's teams.	A	B	C

Eastshire School is introducing a new game this year known as Korfball.

The only facts that are known are that:

- Korfball was invented in 1901 by an Amsterdam schoolmaster, Nico Broekhuysen and is a game a bit like netball and basketball. The difference is that it is played by mixed teams;

- mixed teams are used because Nico wanted a game which could be played by his schoolchildren, both boys and girls. The important aspect was that boys and girls should be able to compete on an equal footing and remain safe;

- it was first played in Holland in 1902, just a few years after James Naismith invented basketball in the USA;

- a national association was formed in the Netherlands in 1903 and soon the game spread to almost 40 other countries, including Armenia, Australia, Belgium, Britain, Germany, India, Indonesia, Portugal, Spain, Japan, Taiwan and the USA;

- the Federation International de Korfball was formed in 1923 but the name was changed to the International Korfball Federation in 1978;

- the IKF is recognised by the International Olympic Committee.

(Based on *What is Korfball?*)

26. Korfball was invented in the eighteenth century in the
    Netherlands.   A   B   C

27. The idea was that girls would have an advantage over boys.   A   B   C

28. It was invented just before basketball came about.   A   B   C

29. It is now played in India, Indonesia, Britain, Austria and Spain. A   B   C

30. Korfball will be a favourite game in Europe following the
    2012 Olympic Games in London.   A   B   C

31. The first official federation for Korfball was established
    22 years after it was invented.   A   B   C

VERBAL LOGICAL REASONING
PRACTICE TEST 6

1.58

There has been a noticeable increase in incidents of disorderly behaviour in Eastshire. The only facts that are known are that:

- a fight broke out in the Spear in Hand pub in Central Eastshire. Three men were taken to hospital injured, one seriously;

- Dan Lewis the pub landlord said, 'Some people came in here just hell-bent on causing trouble. What can you do to prevent it? If trouble is what they want, you can't reason with them, they will just do what they want to anyway';

- Mark Thompson, a sergeant from the Eastshire Police, said, 'In relation to crime, things have become much worse in the centre of Eastshire recently. It is down to a small minority of yobs who are intent on causing as much trouble as they can. They will be dealt with severely, mark my word';

- according to police statistics, incidents of disorder have increased by over 30% in the last three months. Intelligence-led policing is considered imperative by some in the police;

- in an attempt to combat this increase in violent crime and disorder the local police have set up a plain-clothes squad who will be in the pubs waiting for trouble. They will attempt to visit as many pubs as they can;

- according to Inspector John McTavish who set up the squad, 'There has been no shortage of officers volunteering to sit in the pubs, having a drink and looking for trouble. We cannot just be reactive – what is called for is a proactive approach to this problem '.

1. After the fight in the Spear in Hand public house three men were taken to hospital. Two had serious injuries. A B C

2. Dan Lewis highlighted the problem that if people want to enter a pub and find trouble they will, as there is no reasoning with them. A B C

3. Sergeant Mark Thompson observed that crime is on the increase. According to statistics incidents increased by just under 30%. A B C

4. The plain-clothes squad will visit as many pubs as possible, relying on local intelligence to direct their attention. A B C

5. John McTavish highlighted the importance of reacting to trouble.

    A   B   C

Crime is not just restricted to disorder in the public houses; recently there have been some problems with bank cards. The only facts that are known are that:

- at the Rockroses (au) bank (www.rockroses.au), a number of bank cards have been stolen while the owners were trying to access money from their accounts;
- the scam involved taping a black box over the slot where the card is inserted and then waiting for a person to insert the card;
- the unsuspecting customer types in their PIN number while the thief watches. The machine appears not to work;
- the thief advises the customer that they should go into the bank and sort it out; while they are in the bank the thief takes the black box, card and PIN;
- six Eastshire residents have so far been victim to the scam, three in one day. The problem is, explains Superintendent Alison Stuart, the customers are rather too trusting of strangers. They take the advice of the thief, which is just what the thief wants them to do, namely move away so that they can retrieve the card;
- according to the local police, a squad is being disbanded and put into uniform to ensure the police's presence is noticed.

6. Thieves are able to obtain the PIN by applying to the bank.

    A   B   C

7. The scam involves taping a black box to the outside of the cash machine during the hours of darkness.

    A   B   C

8. Superintendent Stuart suggests that in general people are being too trusting in accepting the advice of strangers.

    A   B   C

9. When the person goes into the bank the thief is free to remove the card which they then use with the PIN.

    A   B   C

10. The police are placing more officers in uniform to create a presence.

    A   B   C

Unfortunately the story does not end there; a new scam has emerged where the older members of society are being stolen from. The only facts that are known are that:

- a person knocks on an elderly person's door claiming to be a police officer. They state that someone has tried to use their bank cards fraudulently;
- next they ask for the bank cards which they say will be used for electronic forensic purposes. Next they ask for the PINs, which they record and place in an envelope, this is then sealed in front of the victim;

- the person is asked not to say a thing to anyone about the card as it could jeopardise the case. They then leave and spend the elderly person's money;

- one person lost £20,000, another £12,000 and another £5,000. In all cases this was all the money they had saved. The thieves did not stop until all the money had been spent;

- according to Detective Sergeant Dogberry, 'This is an appalling crime; the thieves seem to have no compassion whatsoever. Substantial amounts of money are being stolen and we get to hear about it sometimes only weeks after. We implore you, if you have an elderly relative or neighbour, let them know about this scam';

- according to the local police a squad is being set up to combat this crime wave.

---

11. The thieves are well organised and prey on the elderly. <u>A</u> B C

12. As a result of the scam the thieves obtain both the card and the PIN. <u>A</u> B C

13. Once the thieves have obtained both the card and the PIN they spend all of the money. <u>A</u> B C

14. In the example given more than £38,000 has been stolen. A <u>B</u> C

15. Sometimes it is a matter of weeks before the police are informed about the crime. <u>A</u> B C

16. The police are asking for relatives and friends of the elderly to let them know about the scam and are offering a substantial reward. A <u>B</u> C

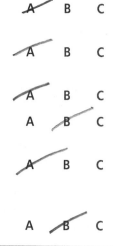

A parking attendant has become the latest victim of road rage in Eastshire. The only facts that are known are that:

- Eastshire Crown Court heard that Donald Bankart, a managing director of a local packaging company, flew into a rage when he found a traffic warden writing out a ticket for him in the town centre;

- he hurled abuse at him before apparently driving off; he then returned in his car and hit the traffic warden, forcing him over the bonnet and on to the roof of his car, the court heard;

- Mr Bankart then drove at speed through the town centre as the traffic warden held onto the car aerial for his life. He only stopped when forced to do so by a school crossing patrol lady;

- Mr Bankart told the court that he had not meant to hurt the traffic warden and it was only because the road was covered in diesel that he was unable to stop. He said that he had not realised that the traffic warden was on his roof and the first he knew about it was when the school crossing patrol lady stopped him to tell him;

- Judge Michael Rowan told Bankart: 'This incident was engendered by what might be termed as road rage but in reality this is a rage against a poor parking attendant.'

(Based on Sky News (2009) *Man jailed over 'parking rage' attack*)

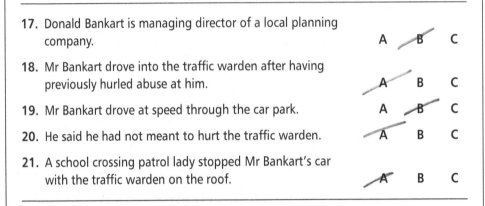

17. Donald Bankart is managing director of a local planning company.   A   B   C

18. Mr Bankart drove into the traffic warden after having previously hurled abuse at him.   A   B   C

19. Mr Bankart drove at speed through the car park.   A   B   C

20. He said he had not meant to hurt the traffic warden.   A   B   C

21. A school crossing patrol lady stopped Mr Bankart's car with the traffic warden on the roof.   A   B   C

Another crime that has hit the streets of Eastshire is that of a nasty drug, crystal meth. The only facts that are known are that:

- police recently discovered a laboratory for producing crystal methamphetamine on a council estate in Eastshire. It was discovered when one of the officers noticed a distinctive smell, similar to cat's urine or burnt rubber. Outside the premises were an unusually high number of discarded cold remedy boxes – both of these are among the signs of crystal meth production;

- two men have been arrested;

- according to government statistics its use in Britain is still relatively unusual. But it is a very destructive substance and is claimed by some to be the most addictive drug in the world;

- the police are so worried about the drug taking hold in the UK that popular flu remedies may soon become prescription-only medications;

- there is increasing concern that pseudoephedrine and ephedrine, found in over-the-counter decongestants, are being extracted to make the drug methyl amphetamine;

- some 12 million Americans are estimated to have used crystal meth, a drug which can be smoked, snorted, swallowed or injected. It greatly heightens sexual arousal but over time mercilessly ravages the body. It is a major problem in Australia, New Zealand, Canada and Japan.

(Based on Midgley, C (2007) Crystal meth: coming to a town near you. *Times Online*)

22. Pseudoephedrine and ephedrine are component parts of methyl amphetamine.

    A   B   C

23. Crystal meth is a major problem in Australia, New Zealand and the UK.

    A   B   C

24. Sales of crystal meth are on the increase in the UK.

    A   B   C

25. The manufacture of crystal meth produces a smell similar to cat urine or burning rubble.

    A   B   C

26. Some 10 million Americans are estimated to have used crystal meth.

    A   B   C

Problems and youths are synonymous according to some in Eastshire, but what do the statistics say about this? The only facts that are known are that:

- figures show that the number of young people killed year-on-year in violent crime is relatively small. The problem for the casual observer is that apparently dramatic changes can be statistically misleading;

- in 1995, 44 people aged between 5 and 16 were victims of homicide. In 2005–06 the number was less than half of that and during the in-between years it varied wildly. In the last year it went up again. The most relevant fact is that almost half of all child victims are killed by a parent;

- interestingly, almost a fifth of all crimes committed by people under the age of 18 are violent offences (second only to theft) and the number of violent crimes has risen consecutively for four years;

- the vast majority of crimes involve minor assaults which, although they are frightening for the victim, can usually be dealt with by warnings from the police;

- of last year's crimes, 39,000 offences were committed by young men and 15,000 by young women;

- the number of offenders will be lower than the number of recorded offences because one person is very often found to have assaulted more than one victim;

- only 1,500 crimes resulted in some form of detention and only nine involved a life detention order.

(Based on Casciani, D. (2008) Analysis: UK gun crime figures. Home affairs reporter BBC News)

27. Less than half of all child victims are killed by a parent.   A   B   C

28. One in four crimes committed by people under the age of 18 is violent.   A   B   C

29. Young women account for less crime than young men but the number of their crimes has risen consecutively for four years.   A   B   C

30. The figures suggest that young men enjoy committing crime.   A   B   C

31. There is a discrepancy between the number of offences and offenders as some people commit more than one offence.   A   B   C

VERBAL LOGICAL REASONING
PRACTICE TEST 7

15 : 23

A move towards religious understanding and tolerance in Eastshire has resulted in the following guidance offered to residents in respect of Buddhism and its religious buildings.

- Buddhism is 500 years older than Christianity and is spread over most of the Far East. It took in all the cultural and religious influences of the countries with which it came into contact.

- At the heart of Buddhist belief are the Three Jewels.

    - I seek Refuge in the Buddha.

    - I seek Refuge in the Dharma.

    - I seek Refuge in the Sangha.

- There are two main traditions of Buddhism. The first is Theravadin which is to be found in Sri Lanka, Burma, Vietnam and Thailand. Here the oldest traditions of devotion and meditation are still adhered to.

- The second tradition of Buddhism is the Mahayana traditions. These have a more complex belief system based on the Bodhissattva but still retain the tradition of meditation as a central act of devotion.

- Buddhist worship is individualist rather than congregational; congregational worship occurs mainly at festival or celebration times.

- Buddhism generally focuses its devotions through meditation; this practice has a significant impact on the style of religious buildings.

(Based on Places of Worship online)

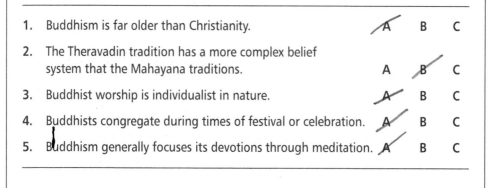

1.	Buddhism is far older than Christianity.	A	B	C
2.	The Theravadin tradition has a more complex belief system that the Mahayana traditions.	A	B	C
3.	Buddhist worship is individualist in nature.	A	B	C
4.	Buddhists congregate during times of festival or celebration.	A	B	C
5.	Buddhism generally focuses its devotions through meditation.	A	B	C

The following guidance was offered to residents in respect of Christianity and its religious buildings.

- England is divided into 43 dioceses. Each of these dioceses has a cathedral at the centre of its worshipping community. Some of the cathedrals are very old indeed, having been in place when monks established them.

- Essentially, a cathedral is a Christian place of worship which has the Bishop's Seat within it – a place where the main clergyperson of a diocese, the bishop, has an opportunity to conduct worship.

- Orthodox Christianity split from the Catholic branch of Christianity about 1054 AD. It is therefore a very old branch of Christianity with many traditions and ceremonies.

- It has become increasingly popular in the UK in recent years owing to large numbers of eastern europeans coming to England for work. The Russian and Greek branches are probably the most influential members.

- Their distinctive differences of belief are in the seven sacraments or mysteries and the veneration of icons or pictures of the saints.

- The most sacred parts of the Orthodox Service are conducted by clergy behind a wooden screen called an Iconostasis. This represents the division between heaven and earth and is painted with figures of Christ, Mary and the saints.

(Based on Places of Worship online)

6.	The majority of the population in the UK are Christian.	A	B	C
7.	The main clergyperson of a diocese is a bishop.	A	B	C
8.	The most sacred parts of the Orthodox Service are the seven mysteries or sacraments.	A	B	C
9.	The wooden screen in the orthodox church is called an Iconostasis.	A	B	C
10.	Orthodox Christianity split from the Catholic branch of Christianity in 1066 following the battle of Hastings.	A	B	C

The following guidance was offered to residents in respect of Hinduism and its religious buildings.

- Hinduism has such a long history in India that it is inevitable that a great diversity within the traditions has emerged. In the UK, Hinduism has had a much shorter time within which to become established; this can be traced back to the 1950s.

- *Puja* is the Hindu term for worship or devotions and it is important for Hindu homes to have a place set aside for *puja* ritual.

- Now traditional Hindu Mandirs (temples) are being built in the UK based on traditional Hindu plans and reflecting the need to serve a much larger faith community.

- Before the construction of a Mandir, the earth on which the building is constructed is blessed and permission sought from the land to disturb its natural state for construction of a Mandir. A small pot is ritually placed in the foundations to symbolise the harmonious relationship between humans and the earth.

- The design of the Mandir is intended to symbolically represent the microcosm of the perfect proportions of creation. No metals are used in the construction as it is believed that metal interferes with the mental efforts needed for meditation and devotion.

- Traditionally, a Mandir will have been built with the front facing the rays from the rising sun. Central to the Mandir however, is the practice of devotions or *puja* to images or Murtis including Ganesh, Vishnu and Krishna.

(Based on Places of Worship online)

---

11. Hinduism is growing in popularity in the UK due to the influx of people from Asia.	A	B	C
12. Punjab is the Hindu term for worship or devotions.	A	B	C
13. Before a Mandir is built permission is sought from the land.	A	B	C
14. It is believed that meditation and devotion can be interfered with by metal.	A	B	C
15. Traditionally, a Mandir will have been built with the front facing the rays from the setting sun.	A	B	C

The following guidance was offered to residents in respect of Islam and its religious buildings.

- 'Islam' means submission (to Allah). Muslims use prostration or bowing to the ground as an act of devotion and as a symbolic action in their prayers and in their worship.

- It is an obligation for Muslims to pray and many Muslims do this five times a day at times specified to them. The word 'mosque' is derived from a word which means 'place of prostration'. Thus the architectural features of a mosque will allow Muslims to prostrate themselves or bow in a form of prayer ritual called a *rakah*.

- No images or pictures of people are to be found in a mosque and, because this has always been the case, traditional designs in a mosque are based on the creativity of Allah in nature and geometric design.

- It is traditional that men and women worship separately. Therefore there will be room available in the mosque for this.

- For a Muslim, from birth the home is central to the learning of the Qu'ran and the sacred language of Islam, Arabic. Texts from the Qu'ran will be on the walls and Muslim prayers as well as verses from the Qu'ran will be learnt by heart. It is also the religious duty of parents to teach their children good manners and this is done through example and instruction.

(Based on Places of Worship online)

---

16. The word 'Islam' means submission (to Allah).   A   B   C

17. The word 'mosque' is derived from a word which
    means 'place of prostration'.   A   B   C

18. Pictures of people are to be found in a mosque.   A   B   C

19. *Rakah* is a form of prayer ritual and is performed
    following *wudu*.   A   B   C

20. Men and women worship separately.   A   B   C

The following guidance was offered to residents in respect of Judaism and its religious buildings.

- In Orthodox Synagogues it was men who traditionally took the greater lead in learning and being able to read in Hebrew. Since the time of the destruction of the Temple in Jerusalem in AD 70, it is the synagogue that has been the central place of learning and worship.

- The Torah Scrolls are the most important and sacred items. Within these writings are to be found the essential teachings and governances by which Jewish people live. Torah Scrolls are housed in an Ark.

- In Orthodox Judaism, the ability to read the Torah Scroll in Hebrew is an important sign of adulthood. The Bimah is the reading stand from which the Torah is read. Services are led from the Bimah and seats are placed in front of it.

- In Orthodox synagogues men and women sit separately.

- Other symbols will also usually be found within the synagogue: the Star of David (or the Magen David) depicts two triangles, one pointing up to heaven, the other pointing to earth, representing the joining of these in the Torah; the *menorah* or seven-branched candlestick is also present; and a light, never extinguished, representing God's presence.

- On Sabbath eve, in the home, it is the mother who prepares the Shabbat meal and setting of the table. It is the mother who lights the two candles to welcome

Shabbat and it is the mother who says the blessing. The mother ensures kosher regulations are observed correctly.

(Based on Places of Worship online)

21. The Torah Scrolls are the most important and sacred items.   A   B   C

22. The Star of David is made up of two triangles pointing west and east.   A   B   C

23. Torah Scrolls are housed in an Ark.   A   B   C

24. The *menorah* or seven-branched candlestick presents a light that is never extinguished.   A   B   C

25. The Sabbath eve is on a Friday evening at 5 p.m.   A   B   C

26. Men and women sit separately in the synagogue.   A   B   C

The following guidance was offered to residents in respect of Sikhism and its religious buildings.

- Sikhism comes originally from the Punjab in North Western India and today the Golden Temple of Amritsar in the Punjab is considered the most sacred of Sikh holy places.

- It is the centrality of the sacred scripture, the Guru Granth Sahib, on the *takht* or throne, that affects the design most. Covered by a canopy, resting on cushions and elevated above the sitting worshippers, the Guru Granth Sahib is regarded with utmost reverence.

- During worship a fly whisk called a *chauri* is waved over the Guru Granth Shahib as a symbolic gesture of the authority of the sacred book.

- Many Gurdwaras are recognisable from the outside by the golden onion-shaped domes. However Gurdwaras in the UK adapted from community buildings will have the Nishan Sahib or Sikh flag identifying them.

- Hospitality, or being able to provide for the comforts of strangers and friends, e.g. by providing food, is a key element in the beliefs of the Sikh community. The provision of food affects the design and architecture of the Gurdwara. The *langar* (kitchen) features prominently beside the Gurdwara.

- Because of the distinctive turban that Sikhs adopt, Sikh men and boys are easily recognisable.

(Based on Places of Worship online)

27. Sikhism comes originally from the Punjab in South East India. A B C

28. A *chauri* is waved over the Guru Granth Shahib as a symbolic gesture of the authority of the sacred book. A B C

29. The Nishan Sahib or Sikh flag is a saffron-coloured triangular-shaped cloth, usually reinforced in the middle with Sikh insignia in blue. A B C

30. A stranger will be fed at a Gurdwara. A B C

31. Sikh women and girls are easily recognisable as they wear turbans. A B C

VERBAL LOGICAL REASONING PRACTICE TEST 8

The Eastshire council is keen to ensure that road traffic collisions are reduced. The following national information is produced for your information.

- This publication includes National Statistics on road casualties in personal injury road accidents reported to the police in Great Britain for the first quarter of 2009, according to the arrangements approved by the UK Statistics Authority.

- The provisional estimates show that the number of fatalities in road accidents were down by 13 per cent for the 12 months ending March 2009, compared to the previous 12 months.

- Total casualties were down by 8 per cent and killed and seriously injured casualties 9 per cent, compared with the previous 12 months.

- Figures for 2009 have been revised slightly since the publication of *Road Casualties in Great Britain 2010*.

- The number of reported seriously injured casualties has increased by 5 per cent to 26,034 and the number of slightly injured casualties has increased by 16 per cent to 202,333.

- Very few, if any, fatal accidents do not become known to the police. However, research conducted on behalf of the Department in the 1990s has shown that a significant proportion of non-fatal injury accidents are not reported to the police.

(Adapted from Department for Transport (2009) *Reported road casualties in Great Britain: Quarterly provisional estimates Q1 2009*)

---

1. This report includes National Statistics on road casualties in personal injury road accidents which are reported to the police.   A   B   C

2. The estimates, which are provisional, indicate that the number of fatalities in road accidents were down by 13 per cent.   A   B   C

3. Very few, if any, fatal accidents do not become known to the police, especially where only one party is involved.   A   B   C

4. The 2009 figures have been revised slightly since the publication of *Road Casualties in Great Britain 2010*.   A   B   C

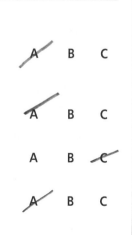

5. Research conducted on behalf of the Department in the 1990s has shown that a significant proportion of non-fatal injury accidents are reported to the police.   A   B   C

The Eastshire council is keen to ensure that crime on public transport is reduced. The following national information is produced for your information.

- Whilst 64% of respondents felt positive about their personal security while travelling, some people can still feel apprehensive. These apprehensions often reflected the respondent's age, gender and ethnic background; for example:

    - men, being more likely to be a victim of violence or robbery, felt more fearful of the presence of groups of other men;

    - women, who were more likely to experience harassment or sexual assault, are more concerned about the behaviour of lone men;

    - younger people were found to be most likely to experience being threatened or stared at in a hostile or intimidating manner;

    - minority ethnic passengers felt further exposed to the wider experience of racial harassment and therefore likely to have concerns, but were less likely to report any incidents;

    - people with disabilities felt particularly vulnerable to the threat of crime where access to transport is limited or via poorly lit, isolated routes.

- The survey also reveals the measures that help passengers feel more secure. People waiting for or travelling by bus for example, felt that locally monitored CCTV surveillance was the most reassuring form of security.

- Those who travelled by train felt that the presence of staff on the platform or collecting tickets on board the train made them feel more secure. In both cases, passengers said that the provision of Help Points, clear signage and improved lighting was particularly welcome.

- Information about services and delays also improves people's comfort. Passengers feel that accurate, real-time information displays and public address systems help them feel more in control of their situation.

- It is also worth noting that people often feel at their most vulnerable during the walk home from the bus or train – especially at night.

(Adapted from Department for Transport (2004) *Tackling crime on public transport*)

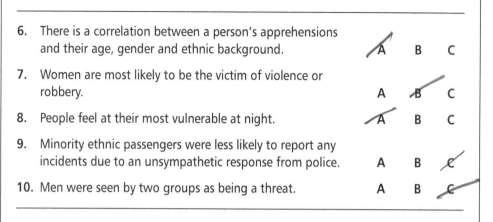

6. There is a correlation between a person's apprehensions and their age, gender and ethnic background.   A   B   C

7. Women are most likely to be the victim of violence or robbery.   A   B   C

8. People feel at their most vulnerable at night.   A   B   C

9. Minority ethnic passengers were less likely to report any incidents due to an unsympathetic response from police.   A   B   C

10. Men were seen by two groups as being a threat.   A   B   C

The Eastshire council is keen to ensure that graffiti on public transport is eradicated. The following New York case study is offered for your consideration.

- Fifteen years ago the stations and carriages of the New York subway were covered with graffiti. Passengers recall not being able to see out of the windows, so complete was the coverage of the graffiti. Today both are completely clear from painted graffiti.

- The New York City Transit subway system operates every day, 24 hours a day, throughout the boroughs of Manhattan, Brooklyn, Queens and the Bronx. The 25 subway lines serve 5.1 million customers on an average weekday and about 1.1 billion passengers a year.

- There are 5,800 carriages, making over 6,000 train trips per day. There are 468 stations, 656 miles of track (not including sidings) and 18 yards where cars are kept overnight. All stations are open 24 hours a day, though some close certain entrances at night, when staffing is also reduced.

- The anti-graffiti initiative on the New York subway dates from 1984, when staff were assigned to the terminals and yards to start cleaning the rolling stock. Those carriages that had a stainless steel exterior had to be completely cleaned; those that were painted had to be painted over. Stations were cleaned, one at a time, and inspected every day to ensure that they stayed clean. Any new 'hit' was cleaned off, or if this was not possible, painted over.

- Recognising that the task was enormous, and that to achieve some early successes it would be important to make a visible impact, the company embarked on a line-by-line approach to cleaning up the system. The first graffiti-free line was the F Line in February 1985. The whole network was finally graffiti-free in May 1989.

(Based on Department for Transport (2006) Case study *New York City: A focused approach to rapid cleaning and removal*)

11. Sixteen years ago the stations and carriages of the New York subway were covered with graffiti.   A   ~~B~~   C

12. The subway comprises of 25 lines, on an average weekday, these serve 5.1 million customers.   ~~A~~   B   C

13. Some entrances close at night.   ~~A~~   B   C

14. The anti-graffiti initiative began in 1984 and took over seven years to complete.   A   ~~B~~   C

15. The first graffiti-free line was the F Line in February 1985 which was followed the following month by the G Line.   A   B   ~~C~~

16. New Yorkers are delighted with the scheme.   A   B   ~~C~~

The Eastshire council is keen to ensure that young people carried on public transport do not commit crime. The following research is offered for your consideration.

- The relationship between young people and bus personnel has been problematic. Bus drivers see young people as a major source of stress and damage.

- Trying to drive a bus whilst taking responsibility for the welfare of up to 80 young people, some of whom will be engaged in behaviour ranging from the high spirited (e.g. running up and down the stairs) to the wilfully life-threatening (e.g. interfering with the emergency exit), can put intolerable strain on staff.

- This strain is frequently compounded by drivers' perceptions that, not only are they powerless to take effective measures, but disruptive children are aware of this. Anecdotal evidence would indicate a deteriorating situation.

- Children, for their part, believe that their custom is not valued by the bus companies or their staff. Complaints from schoolchildren about poor-quality buses, overcrowding, and surly service are frequent. They perceive the majority of bus drivers to be unsympathetic.

- Bus drivers dread the school run. Schoolchildren, the future customer base of public transport, are being turned off bus travel before they have become economically active. This was the backdrop against which the Department of the Environment, Transport, and the Regions commissioned Crime Concern to research, develop and pilot training designed to improve driver skills in managing the situation.

- Early in our research it became apparent that an approach to the problem based solely on training drivers had poor prospects for success. Driver behaviour was likely to be a significant factor, but so too were the perceptions schoolchildren had about acceptable behaviour on buses. Furthermore, even if the perceptions each group had of the other could be improved and relations put on a more positive footing, progress could be sabotaged without co-operation and support from schools.

(From the Department for Transport (2004) *The school run. A training programme for bus drivers focusing on conflict resolution with school pupils*)

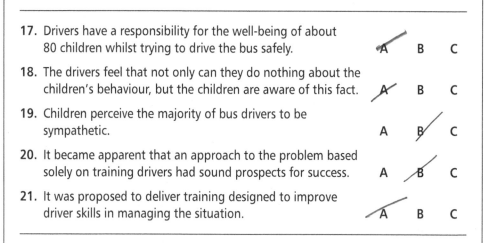

17. Drivers have a responsibility for the well-being of about 80 children whilst trying to drive the bus safely. A B C

18. The drivers feel that not only can they do nothing about the children's behaviour, but the children are aware of this fact. A B C

19. Children perceive the majority of bus drivers to be sympathetic. A B C

20. It became apparent that an approach to the problem based solely on training drivers had sound prospects for success. A B C

21. It was proposed to deliver training designed to improve driver skills in managing the situation. A B C

The Eastshire council is keen to ensure that taxi and PHV drivers are safe whilst engaged in their work. Part 1 of the following research is offered for your consideration.

The scale and type of incidents faced by taxi and PHV drivers.

- Problems could be caused by anyone, although given the high demand for taxis and PHV in town and city centres late at night, many of those causing the problems will be younger rather than older people. Increasing numbers of women are said to cause problems for the driver.

- *Violent offences* – Drivers are subjected to assaults and robbery. On average, three drivers a year are unlawfully killed. The emotional and physical impact of some incidents is so severe that the victim has stopped working as a taxi or private-hire driver.

- Drivers are more at risk of attack or robbery in isolated locations. Some attacks on drivers are premeditated: perpetrators set out to rob the drivers and use violence to achieve their objective.

- *Bilking or non payment of fares* – If drivers take action to prevent passengers from running off without paying it can make them vulnerable to abuse, robbery or violence.

- *Racist abuse* – Asian and other minority ethnic drivers appear to be subject to higher levels of abuse and much of this is racist in content. Very few of these incidents are reported to the police.

(From the Department for Transport (2007) *Research on the personal security issues for taxi and PHV drivers – Executive summary*)

22. Now, more women than men cause problems for taxi drivers.   A   B   ~~C~~

23. On average three drivers are killed for their takings each year.   ~~A~~   B   C

24. Some attacks are premeditated and involve robbery.   ~~A~~   B   C

25. Taking action against a bilker reduces violence.   A   ~~B~~   C

26. Racist abuse is rarely reported to police.   ~~A~~   B   C

The Eastshire council is keen to ensure that taxi and PHV drivers are safe whilst engaged in their work. Part 2 of the following research is offered for your consideration.

- Night-time is the period when most of the problems occur, many associated with the late-night economy. There is a consensus that problems can happen anywhere, but are most likely within major towns and cities. However, it is not in the busy city or town centres that problems are most likely to occur but on route to the destination or at the end of a journey, when a driver is very much on his or her own.

- There are neighbourhoods that are felt to be less safe for drivers, but the problems are said to be caused by only a small minority and usually at specific localities within those areas.

- Drivers always work alone, and often work late into the night when the risks are usually higher and they are known to carry cash. Plying for hire on the street makes a taxi driver more vulnerable because there is no information readily available to the driver about the person or persons that he or she is picking up.

- The problems faced by drivers are closely associated with alcohol misuse. The pressure is on the police and others to clear town and city centres as quickly as possible at the end of the night, and this can mean drivers are told to take customers that are very drunk and whom they would rather refuse to carry.

- Dealing with situations where customers have taken illegal drugs is far more difficult for drivers. The use of illegal drugs is said to be increasing as a contributing factor to criminal and antisocial incidents.

(From the Department for Transport (2007) *Research on the personal security issues for taxi and PHV drivers – Executive summary*)

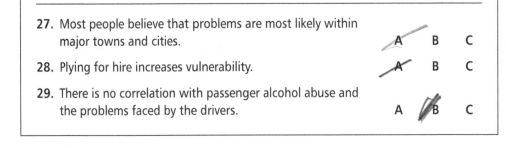

27. Most people believe that problems are most likely within major towns and cities.   ~~A~~   B   C

28. Plying for hire increases vulnerability.   ~~A~~   B   C

29. There is no correlation with passenger alcohol abuse and the problems faced by the drivers.   A   ~~B~~   C

30. The police are adding to the problem by expecting the drivers to take drunk people home: they are then assaulted by the drunk passengers.

    A   B   C

31. It is easier for the drivers to deal with people who have taken a combination of drugs and alcohol.

    A   B   C

VERBAL LOGICAL REASONING PRACTICE TEST 9

Concerns have been voiced amongst some member of the Eastshire community in relation to the use of guns by gangs. The following is representative of the national situation.

- London, the West Midlands, Greater Manchester and Nottingham account for more than half of recorded gun crime in England and Wales. In 2004–2005, 34 per cent of recorded gun crime occurred in London, at a rate of 50 offences per 100,000 people. Between April 2001 and October 2005, 63 per cent of victims of murder and attempted murder involving firearms in London were black.

- 'Gun crime is mainly committed by young men aged 16–25. Offenders and victims are getting younger and a disproportionate number are African Caribbeans,' according to the Metropolitan Police. Shotguns can cost as little as £50 to £200.

- There is an emergence of 'disorganised' as opposed to organised criminals using firearms to settle relatively trivial disputes, especially in 'the street-level economy'. The illegal drug market remains the single most important theme in relation to the use of illegal firearms, but gang membership and the need to emulate successful criminals are also important factors.

- Gangs or 'crews' are formed typically from close friendship groups based around a school or neighbourhood and offer members safety in numbers. In south London, crews in key areas such as Brixton, Peckham and New Cross have territories that include housing estates and shopping centres.

- Internal rivalries, notions of 'dis' (disrespect), and drug raids by the police all destabilise gang structures and can inflame violence.

- Even quite trivial disputes can result in shootings because the presence of guns aggravates threats and makes pre-emptive attacks more likely: the so-called 'shoot or be shot' scenario.

(Based on Ford, R. (2007) The facts of Britain's gun culture. *Times Online*)

---

1. Five areas of the UK account for more than half of recorded gun crime in England and Wales.   A   B   C

2. Between April 2001 and October 2005 the majority of gun crime victims were white and Asian.   A   B   C

3. According to the Metropolitan Police, shotguns can cost as little as £40.   A   B   C

4. Drug raids by the police destabilise gang structures and can inflame violence so should be avoided.   A   B   C

5. The presence of guns aggravates threats and makes pre-emptive attacks more likely.   A   B   C

The Home Office was consulted by the Eastshire committee for an informed view of the gun crime situation. The following is representative of the national situation.

• The number of overall offences involving firearms fell by 2% in 2007–08 compared to the previous year. Firearms were involved in 455 serious or fatal injuries, compared to 468 the previous year – a drop of 3%. Offences involving handguns effectively held steady, those involving shotguns were down 3%. The number of reported crimes involving imitation guns effectively held steady.

• The Home Office has:

  – introduced a minimum five-year sentence for people convicted of possessing an illegal firearm;

  – made it an offence to possess an air weapon or imitation firearm in public without legal authority or reasonable excuse;

  – increased the age limit for possession of air rifles to 17;

  – prohibited certain air weapons that are easily converted to fire live ammunition.

• The Violent Crime Reduction Act 2006:

  – targets imitation firearms – by making it illegal to manufacture or sell imitation firearms that could be mistaken for real firearms, strengthening sentences for carrying imitation firearms, and creating tougher manu-facturing standards so imitations can't be converted to fire real ammunition;

  – reduces illegal use of air weapons – by increasing the age limit for buying or firing air weapons without supervision;

  – they are cutting off the supply of firearms into the country by tightening security on import routes and international mail, and monitoring online firearm suppliers.

(From the Home Office (2009) *Crime and victims. Gun crime*)

---

6. From 2007 to 2008 gun crime has not really improved. The Government's own statistics show a reduction of just 2%.   A   B   C

7. Firearms involved in serious or fatal injuries reduced by a total of 13 from 2007 to 2008.   A   B   C

8. The Home Office has introduced a maximum five-year sentence for people convicted of possessing an illegal firearm.   A   B   C

esibire ?!

9. The Home Office has exhibited certain air weapons that
are easily converted to fire live ammunition.   A   B   C

10. The Violent Crime Reduction Act 2006 makes it legal to
manufacture firearms that could be mistaken for real
firearms.   A   B   C

The Home Office has launched an initiative which the Eastshire council may consider.
What is known about this is that:

- a new funding stream to support community organisations working to tackle
guns, gangs and knife crime has now been launched. The Home Office's £4.5m
Community Fund is helping the community tackle guns, gangs and knives;

- youth violence is a major problem that continues to devastate families, communities and neighbourhoods;

- the Home Office is working across government to provide help and support for
young people, parents and victims. Voluntary and community organisations are
key to this process and can make a real difference by transforming the lives of
vulnerable young people who are either at risk or who have been involved in
gangs;

- the Home Secretary outlined a new £4.5m fund for local community groups to
run activities for young people in 13 priority areas;

- this will fund intensive work with young people through mentoring and outreach
work. Organisations can apply for grant funding of up to £10,000 per annum for
three years;

- this fund is being managed on behalf of the Home Office by Tribal's Community
Development Team.

(Based on Connected (2009))

---

11. The Home Office's £45m Community Fund is helping the
community tackle guns, gangs and knives.   A   B   C

12. Youth violence is a major problem that continues to
devastate inner-city families, communities and
neighbourhoods.   A   B   C

13. Voluntary and community organisations are unlikely to
assist this process without the aid of the Home Office. A   B   C

14. Organisations can apply for grant funding of up to
£1,000 per annum for three years.   A   B   C

15. This fund is being managed on behalf of the Home
Office by Tribal's Community Development Team, which
is a subsidiary of the department for UK Resilience.   A   B   C

The second Connected conference (Part 1) highlights issues from which the Eastshire council may benefit. What is known about this is that:

- the Connected 2 event on 24 May 2006 was part of the Home Office's continuing programme of work, policy development and initiatives to tackle gun, gang and knife crime in England and Wales;

- the day brought together 150 people, from the public and voluntary sectors and affected communities, to pool their collective experience and expertise;

- the emotional, educational, practical and spiritual needs of young people were a central focus of the day. Participants emphasised that a broad education, including social, academic, professional and behavioural skills, is essential. Support needs to be available to young people and their families to increase their life chances and reduce their risk of offending;

- violent video games, internet sites, films and lyrics were thought to influence some young people, and increase the attraction of a violent and criminal lifestyle. However, some participants argued that music in particular could be a force for good. Genres such as rap offer opportunities for self expression, creatively channelling aggression and disseminating positive messages;

- very little progress can be made without the support of the community. Engaging the community is critical to success in tackling guns, gangs and knives; and direct community involvement in the design and realisation of strategies and groundwork can significantly strengthen progress;

- social deprivation was considered to be a key risk factor for gang membership. Once empowered, communities – and individuals – can become their own agents for change.

(Based on Connected (2006) *The second Connected conference: Building on our work together to tackle guns, knives and gang-related crime in England and Wales*)

---

16. The Connected 2 event on 24 May 2006 brought
together 150 people.   A   B   C

17. Support needs to be available to young people, their
families, friends and the community to increase their life
chances and reduce their risk of offending.   A   B   C

18. Some forms of music offers opportunities for self
expression, creatively channelling aggression and
disseminating positive messages.   A   B   C

19. Social deprivation was considered to be a key risk factor for gang membership, with unemployment making a critical contribution.   A   B   ~~C~~

20. Much progress can be made without the support of the community.   A   ~~B~~   C

The second Connected conference (Part 2) highlights issues from which the Eastshire council may benefit. What is known about this is that:

- Government departments and services need to work more closely together and ensure that their policies and practice nationally and locally support anti-gang, anti-gun and anti-knife activity;

- in particular, more attention needs to be paid to prevention, by eradicating social deprivation, improving the education and prison systems, and helping people (particularly offenders) get into skilled employment;

- some participants felt that personal faith and the Christian church offer the guiding values, self belief and compassion that are missing from many people's lives. Prayer can be used to change individual and collective behaviour. The church was called upon to engage young people and work more closely with both grassroots organisations and other faiths;

- given the range of people who participated, it is not surprising that there were different views on the nature of the problem and possible solutions. Nonetheless, there was general agreement on three issues:

  - young people must be offered meaningful and appealing opportunities in education, employment and leisure;

  - all national government departments and agencies should work closely together to reduce gun, gang and knife crime, and address its consequences;

  - communities must be involved in developing and implementing plans and activities locally and nationally;

- the ideas, passion, analysis and actions need to continue across the country in every community, in every street, in every home, in every place of worship, in every club, in every school, in every public service – indeed in every place where people hope or dream, fear or lose faith, play or work, or where people just want a better future for their family, friends and neighbours;

- network-building and information-sharing provide a foundation for greater awareness, improved interventions and, ultimately, better lives for individuals and communities.

(Based on Connected (2006) *The second Connected conference: Building on our work together to tackle guns, knives and gang-related crime in England and Wales*)

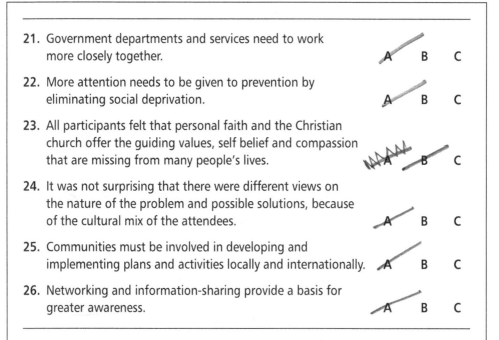

21. Government departments and services need to work more closely together.   A   B   C

22. More attention needs to be given to prevention by eliminating social deprivation.   A   B   C

23. All participants felt that personal faith and the Christian church offer the guiding values, self belief and compassion that are missing from many people's lives.   A   B   C

24. It was not surprising that there were different views on the nature of the problem and possible solutions, because of the cultural mix of the attendees.   A   B   C

25. Communities must be involved in developing and implementing plans and activities locally and internationally.   A   B   C

26. Networking and information-sharing provide a basis for greater awareness.   A   B   C

The Eastshire council contacted Crimestoppers for further information in relation to gun crime. What is known about this is that:

- a children's charity has found that one in ten youths have been personally affected by gun and knife crime and 20% feel they are sometimes or often in danger;

- NCH studied 800 people aged under 25 over a six-month period. The study, called 'Step Inside Our Shoes: Young People's Views on Gun and Knife Crime', recommended that young people need access to more community-based youth services and structured activities;

- 36% of the young people had fears about crime in their area;

- while 15% had been affected by gun and knife crime personally, 41% knew someone who had been affected;

- NCH have called for under-16s to be included in official national crime surveys, so that the extent to which young people are victims can be better understood;

- Crimestoppers is an independent charity and not part of the police. If you wish to pass on information about crime anonymously, please call Crimestoppers on 0800 555 111, or fill out our anonymous online Giving Information Form.

(Based on Crimestoppers (2008) *One in ten young people affected by guns and knives*)

27. A children's charity has found that one in ten youths have been personally affected by gun and knife crime and that this is having a direct effect on their education.　　　A　　B　　C

28. A recent study has recommended that young people need access to more community-based youth services and structured activities, which will reduce gun crime by approximately 15%.　　　A　　B　　C

29. While 15% had been affected by gun and knife crime personally, 14% knew someone who had been affected.　　　A　　B　　C

30. NCH have called for under-14s to be included in official national crime surveys, so that the extent that young people are victims can be better understood.　　　A　　B　　C

31. Crimestoppers is an independent charity and part of the police.　　　A　　B　　C

(Based on Crimestoppers (2008) *One in ten young people affected by guns and knives*)

VERBAL LOGICAL REASONING
PRACTICE TEST 10

The following accounts are taken from actual incidents experienced by police officers in the United Kingdom.

- While on the way to another incident a sergeant saw a woman run towards his car, shouting for help. She was being chased by a man who was carrying a heavy object in his right hand. As the sergeant passed them he saw the man hit the woman over the head, and got out of his car to help her.

- The man tried to hit him with the object, so the sergeant discharged the contents of his CS canister at the man, who then ran into a nearby house. The sergeant saw the man appear at the first-floor window, pointing what he believed to be a shotgun at him, so he radioed for immediate assistance and firearms support. Firearms officers responded and headed for the scene.

- The Control Room Inspector granted immediate firearms authority, assuming the role of Silver Commander, and the firearms officers moved to assemble at a rendezvous point close to the incident.

- The Force's on-call commander for firearms incidents ratified the firearms authority shortly afterwards and began to make his way from home to the scene of the incident. In line with Force policy, he declared himself Silver Commander despite being some distance from the scene, and having no direct radio communication with either the control room or officers at the scene.

- On arrival, the armed officers cordoned off the address and began negotiating. Shortly afterwards the man punched a hole in the upstairs window with his fist and raised a weapon that looked like a shotgun at the armed officers.

- Officers called to the man to drop the weapon, but he refused. One of the armed officers fired a single shot at the man and he disappeared from view. Officers forced entry to the house and found the man lying in a bedroom with a home-made firearm beside him. He was taken to hospital, but was pronounced dead on arrival.

(From NPIA (2008) *Learning the lessons* Bulletin 7)

---

1. The sergeant was on the way to another incident when he
    saw the woman being chased by the man.   A   B   C

2. The sergeant discharged the contents of his CS canister at
    the man.   A   B   C

3.	The CS spray had no effect on the man.	A B C	
4.	The Force's on-call commander for firearms incidents declared himself Silver Commander.	A B C	
5.	A Smith and Wesson firearm was found next to the man.	A B C	

- A young man of 19 was reported missing by his parents in the early hours one Sunday morning. The call operator correctly marked the incident log as 'concern for welfare' but did not record a risk assessment on the incident log.

- An officer attending at the parents' address later that morning graded the incident as low risk on the basis of the information provided. This was done using the Force's hard-copy missing-person form that merely required the officer to tick boxes and not to offer a full rationale for his decision. Because the risk was considered 'low', he did not take down verbatim the text of an answer-phone message left by the young man after his disappearance. It was later deleted.

- The incident was correctly upgraded to 'medium risk' later that day as the young man had still not been in contact. On Monday a reviewing inspector maintained the risk at 'medium', in accordance with the relevant policy and gave a full rationale for his decision.

- By the time another inspector took over the case later that evening there were good reasons to upgrade the case to 'high risk' – the time lapse, the fact that the young man's car had by then been found abandoned with his mobile phone inside and early financial investigations showing no activity on his bank account. The incident was then upgraded to 'high risk' on Thursday.

- Throughout, both the handwritten missing-person form and the computer-generated incident log were used to record enquiries. However, some enquiries and facts were recorded only on the computer-generated incident log.

- About two and a half weeks later, the young man's body was found washed up on a beach. An inquest verdict of suicide was recorded. He probably died before the police were informed.

(From NPIA (2008) *Learning the lessons* Bulletin 7)

6.	A young man of 19 was reported missing by his parents in the early hours one Monday morning.	A B C	
7.	An officer first graded the incident as low risk, having visited the parents.	A B C	
8.	On Monday a reviewing inspector maintained the medium risk.	A B C	

9. The case was later up graded to high risk due solely to the
    fact that the young man's car had been found abandoned.   A   B   C

10. The young man's body was found washed up on a beach,
    he had drowned.   A   B   C

- A woman who had a history of paranoid schizophrenia leading to violence spent
  several spells in hospital. She moved to another area and in June 2006 was
  detained in a psychiatric hospital under Section 3 of the Mental Health Act 1983,
  meaning treatment was considered necessary for her health or safety or for the
  protection of others.

- In the summer of 2006 she deteriorated mentally and physically. One day she
  went missing and after a fruitless search the hospital called the police mid-
  morning, telling them she had been admitted under Section 3 but not apparently
  giving them other information to suggest she presented a risk.

- The call-handler graded the incident as routine, requiring a response within 24
  hours or as soon as possible. This was strictly in accordance with Force guidance
  on risk assessment; however, Force policy required a grading of priority/early
  response (within 30 minutes) for anyone extremely vulnerable or where safety was
  concerned and the risk should have been assessed as high on the information
  available.

- Police did not go to the hospital until nearly 8 p.m. At the hospital, officers noted
  that the missing woman was a paranoid schizophrenic, suffered delusions, had a
  history of violence and was aggressive towards people in uniform.

- Despite this and although she had:
  - been detained under Section 3;
  - been missing for over 8 hours;
  - not contacted her family;
  - and despite that fact that it was evening, they assessed her as medium risk.
    This assessment was later confirmed by an on-duty inspector, in part on the
    basis that she had been missing in the past and returned safely.

- The next morning the police were called to a house in the area, where they
  discovered the woman with a dead man. He had been stabbed. She was charged
  with murder and made subject to an indefinite hospital order.

(From NPIA (2008) *Learning the lessons* Bulletin 5)

11. Section 3 of the Mental Health Act 1983 enables police to detain an individual, only if it is considered necessary for the person's health.   A   B   C

12. In the winter of 2006 the woman deteriorated mentally and physically.   A   B   C

13. At the hospital officers noted that she was aggressive towards people wearing uniform.   A   B   C

14. When considering the assessment, the on-duty inspector took into consideration the fact that she had returned safely in the past.   A   B   C

15. The schizophrenic woman killed the man.   A   B   C

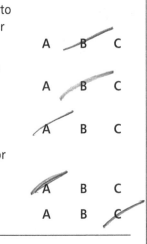

- A young woman arrested for theft had drugs and suicide markers against her name. She told the custody officer she suffered from claustrophobia and was placed in the holding cell, with a requirement for constant observation.

- She was seen throwing herself on the floor and crying. She told officers that she would 'do something' and would not be there much longer. In case she harmed herself an officer was stationed just outside the holding cell and medical assistance requested.

- She was considered fit to be detained, charged with theft and remanded in custody to appear in court two days later. The next morning, she was seen lying on the floor in pain and said she could not stand. The custody officer decided to leave the holding cell door wide open in case there was an emergency before the doctor arrived.

- The doctor examined her and said that she was still fit to be detained. When the doctor was leaving, the custody officer told him the code for the door, not realising the detainee could overhear.

- When she was brought back to the holding cell after the medical examination, the custody assistant closed the door to the holding cell but left it unlocked so that the officer observing her could get immediate access if needed. However, he did not tell either the custody officer or the observing officer that the cell door was unlocked.

- About an hour later, the observing officer went to the toilet and while he was away, the detainee walked out of the holding cell. An officer coming into the custody suite saw her but thought she was a member of the Addiction team based in the station. The detainee grabbed the closing door, then used the code she had overheard to open the second door and escape.

(From NPIA (2008) *Learning the lessons* Bulletin 6)

16. The young woman had previous convictions for theft
    and drug dealing.   A   B   ~~C~~

17. An officer was stationed outside the holding cell because
    of her behaviour.   ~~A~~   B   C

18. The following day she was unable to stand.   A   ~~B~~   C

19. The detainee saw the code for the door written on a
    piece of paper.   A   ~~B~~   C

20. The Addiction team includes drug addicts.   A   B   ~~C~~

- A man of 23 had been convicted of indecent assault on three children when he was 13. He was registered as a sex offender and given a Community Rehabilitation Order (CRO). He was referred to Multi-Agency Public Protection Arrangements (MAPPA).

- Over two years, he was the subject of ten reviews. During this period he was suspected of, arrested for, or charged with a number of serious offences, some with a sexual aspect, including one at a youth club and one involving a minor. The risk assessments made by the police for the Multi-Agency Risk Assessment Committee (MARC) did not always seem to reflect these incidents and, when the risk assessment did change, the MARC minutes did not give any reason.

- A MARC review on the transfer of the sex offender from one force district to another when he changed addresses did not contain the detailed assessment that is required on transfer from one force to another. The charge for one of the most serious offences was dropped, in part because of lack of forensic evidence. However, the reason for discounting two possible pieces of evidence was not recorded.

- The alleged offence involving a minor was not referred to the National Violent and Sex Offenders Register (ViSOR) database or passed to Social Services and officers who knew the man was suspected did not arrest him or seize potential evidence when making a home visit. He told them at the time that he was working in youth hostels elsewhere in the country; they did not follow this up, so missed that he was living for periods at one of the hostels.

- One morning a woman's body was found floating in a canal. CCTV footage showed the man following her from a pub the previous night before returning to the youth hostel where he was living. He was convicted of her murder.

(From NPIA (2008) *Learning the lessons* Bulletin 4)

---

21. A man of 23 had been convicted of indecent assault when
    he was 12 years old.   A   B   C

22. Over ten years, he was the subject of two reviews.   A   B   C

23. He was suspected of, arrested for, or charged with
    committing a number of offences, one at a youth club
    with a minor.   A   B   C

24. The charge for one of the most serious offences was
    dropped, in part because of lack of forensic evidence.   A   B   C

25. ViSOR stands for the Violent and Sex Offenders Register. A   B   C

26. The man killed the woman floating in the canal.   A   B   C

- A woman called police threatening to jump from the twelfth floor of her block of flats. She had had behavioural problems and had been treated over the years for drug and alcohol problems. She also had a history of self-harm, including attempts to hang herself and to set fire to herself.

- When the police arrived they saw her sitting on the balcony with her legs over the wall. An officer struck up a rapport with her and was able to snatch her back from the wall.

- The officers considered whether to detain her under Section 136 of the Mental Health Act 1983 in order to take her to hospital as a place of safety. However, she told them she had called the police because she wanted an audience and agreed to go to hospital voluntarily.

- Early the next morning she called the police and threatened to jump from the balcony again. An inspector found her on the balcony, took hold of her and led her back down to her flat.

- Half an hour later, the woman called the police, again threatening to jump. Officers forced entry to her flat and found her sitting on the window sill with her legs outside, drinking a can of lager.

- She appeared to be drunk and told them she would jump if they came closer. They kept trying to talk to her but about ten minutes after they arrived she jumped from the window. She died from her injuries.

(From NPIA (2008) *Learning the lessons* Bulletin 6)

---

27. The woman lived on the twelfth floor of a block of flats. A   B   C

28. She explained that she had called the police because she
    wanted an audience.   A   B   C

29. In total she threatened to jump from the balcony on four occasions.

A ~~B~~ C

30. On the third occasion she was drinking a can of lager.

~~A~~ B C

31. She jumped five minutes after the police arrived.

A ~~B~~ C

Part 2

The numerical reasoning test

Chapter 3
Introduction to the numerical reasoning test

OBJECTIVES

By the end of this chapter you will be able to:

• recognise the structure of the numerical reasoning test.

Introduction

As explained earlier, it makes sense to be tested on your verbal reasoning skills but perhaps you wonder why a numeracy test is also included in the selection process. However, there are many occasions when, as a police officer, you will be expected to use your numeracy skills. If, for example, a wallet or purse that has been lost is handed to you, you will be expected to count the money accurately and record it before storing it in a safe place. Or, when someone has been arrested, any money they carry, as well as the number of perhaps stolen items, will be counted. Further, if a person is involved with an acquisitional type of crime (theft etc.), you will be expected to identify exactly the numbers and amounts concerned. In some cases these can be quite substantial; for instance, people involved with selling drugs characteristically carry large amounts of money. Numeracy also plays a significant part in other police duties, for example traffic. When prosecuting an individual for a speeding offence it is useful to recognise that speed equals time over distance. The more specialist accident investigation relies heavily on numeracy when working out the route and position of vehicles prior to impact, the accurate measuring of associated marks on the road, e.g. striation marks etc., and measurements of the final position of vehicles and casualties. Also, if your duties involve driving a police vehicle, you will be expected, at the end of your tour of duty, to work out how many miles you have accounted for in that vehicle.

Further, the ability to account for time is also an important factor evidentially. On some occasions a case has been lost when it has been proven by the defence team that the actions of an individual described by an officer could not possibly have taken place in the time suggested. Time is an important consideration when making an arrest, including the time the incident took place, when you (the police) arrived at the scene, when an arrest was made, the time of arrival at the police station and later the time allowed to detain the person under PACE (Police and Criminal Evidence Act 1984).

From the above it is apparent that the ability to perform basic numeracy skills is an essential quality of a modern police officer as the use of mathematics can be found in many everyday police activities.

The nature of the numerical reasoning test

The numerical reasoning test is designed to test your ability to complete basic numerical problems, without the use of a calculator. It forms part of the problem-solving competency which you are tested against on a number of occasions during the assessment centre. For each question there are four possible answers of which only one will be correct. As with the verbal reasoning test, you indicate your chosen response on an answer sheet provided. Any pressure comes from the fact that there are 25 questions to complete in only 12 minutes. Cox (2007) advises that you indentify the halfway point and then ensure you are near that point at the six-minute stage; that is, around question 12 to 13.

Starting your numeracy skills practice here, you will have worked out that you have 28.8 seconds per question (convert 12 minutes into seconds, then divide the seconds by 25. So, $12 \times 60 = 720$; $720 \div 25 = 28.8$). Remember that the difference between a difficult question and an easy one is that you know the answer to the easy one. By familiarising yourself with the basic numeric principles you will change difficult questions into easy ones. Numeracy is much like any other skill: the more you do, the easier it will become.

The answer sheet for the numerical test will be provided and will take the form of the letters:

Ⓐ   Ⓑ   Ⓒ   Ⓓ

You should select only one for each question, by colouring in the circle that corresponds to your answer. The result of the test is given a grade from A to D.

Chapter 4

Understanding basic numeric rules and operations

OBJECTIVES

By the end of this chapter you will be able to:

- identify the basic numeric rules;
- apply these rules in calculations.

The basic numeric rules and operations

This chapter explains the basic numeric rules, giving detailed examples and tasks for you to practise. The answers to the tasks can be found at the end of the book. The test usually contains questions about the following:

1. Addition
2. Subtraction
3. Multiplication
4. Division
5. Averages
6. Percentages
7. Fractions
8. Area and perimeter
9. Volume
10. Time

You are not allowed to use a calculator in the test so, as you practise, get into the habit of using pen and paper to work out sums.

There are different methods to work out some calculations; however, this book offers only one method per topic. If you use a different method and it works for you, please do not feel that you have to use the method suggested within this text: the most important thing is that you pass the numerical test; no one will worry about how you went about it, there is no set rule.

4.1 Addition

This form of numeracy tests your ability to combine numbers to arrive at a total. The sign for addition is +, which is referred to as the plus sign. Language used for addition varies, even though it means the same. For instance you may come across: *x* add *y*; *x* and *y*; *x* plus *y*.

In its most simple form addition is represented as:

1 + 1 = 2 (Don't expect it to be quite so simple in the test.)

There is a standard method when adding numbers. The easiest way to start is to separate the numbers into units (U), tens (T), hundreds (H), thousands (T) etc. For example, 358 can be separated into 8 units, 5 tens and 3 hundreds (always start from the right, with the units). These smaller numbers are easier to deal with when working without a calculator.

TASK 1

Separate the following numbers into units, tens, hundreds, thousands, ten thousands, hundred thousands, etc.:

49	(forty-nine)
274	(two hundred and seventy-four)
2211	(two thousand, two hundred and eleven)
63503	(sixty-three thousand, five hundred and three)
271959	(two hundred and seventy-one thousand, nine hundred and fifty-nine)

Next, when adding numbers together, put the numbers into columns, making sure that the units are underneath the units, the tens underneath the tens, etc.

For example:

358 + 274

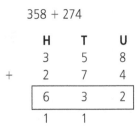

Now you can add the numbers much more easily, as you are working with smaller numbers. Explanation:

TASK 1 continued

Starting from the right with the units column:

8 add 4 equals 12.

2 goes under the units column and the 1, representing 10, is placed under the next column (tens), being 'carried forward'.

Next, the tens column:

5 and 7 are 12; and add the 1 you carried forward, making 13.

The 3 is written under the tens column and the 1 carried forward to the hundreds column.

Finally, the hundreds column:

3 and 2 are 5; and add the 1 which you carried over, making 6.

Your final answer to this sum is therefore: 632

There may be other ways to go about addition but this method works. The principle remains the same, regardless of how many numbers you add together: always separate the numbers into units, tens, hundreds, thousands etc., being accurate in your columns (units under units, tens under tens etc.)

$$92.9992+$$
$$87.467u+$$
$$23.89\,44t$$
$$87.9266=$$

TASK 2

Complete the following addition sums

$$180652 \quad 292287b$$

1.	2.	3.	4.	5.	6.
23	359	311	1010	39378	929992
+ 48	+ 354	943	101	3398	874674
71	713	+ 99	1101	38888	238944
		13 53	+ 1011	+ 98988	+ 879266
			3223	17652	2922886

When you deal with a decimal point when adding up, the decimal point must never move. The numbers are now classified as before, hundreds, tens, units, but with the addition of tenths, hundredths and so on:

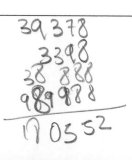

$$39378+$$
$$3398+$$
$$38\,888+$$
$$98\,988=$$
$$180652$$

$$39378$$
$$3398$$
$$38\,888$$
$$989888$$
$$170552$$

TASK 2 continued

For example:

358.75 + 274.25

	H	T	U	.	Th	Hth
	3	5	8	.	7	5
+	2	7	4	.	2	5
	6	3	3	.	0	0
	1	1	1		1	

The method for adding the numbers remains the same; however, it is important to ensure that the decimal point does not wander: placing the numbers in columns assists this.

TASK 3

Complete these:

1.	2.	3.	4.	5.	6.
0.3	0.004	2.834	33.25	1000.0001	101099.9
+ 0.2	+ 1.004	2.834	34.25	2000.0002	27.4
0.5	1.008	+ 2.854	34.25	1000.0009	454545.0005
		8.522	+ 32.50	+ 1000.0003	1.1
			13 4 15	4 000.0015	+ 1.1
			134.25		15
					555673.4005

If you are using pen and paper to work out your answer then be sure to set the numbers out carefully, keeping the decimal points aligned. Using the decimal point correctly is also useful when dealing with money. Try the following:

TASK 4

1.	2.	3.	4.	5.
£ 0.55	£ 9.04	£ 15.99	£ 589.50	£ 1,000,000.00
+ £ 0.55	+ £ 1.03	£ 16.99	£ 989.25	£ 2,000,000.00
1.10	10.07	+ £ 20.99	£ 978.25	£ 100,000.00
		53.97	+ £ 936.50	+ £ 1,000.00
			363.50	3101000.00

If you feel that you require practice adding up with money, then the next time you go shopping at the supermarket, keep a running total, either in your head or on paper, of the amount you have spent.

Brain workout 1

It was mentioned that the more you use your brain the easier thinking will become. There are a number of different ways the brain operates, dependent on the function for which it is used at any time. It may be some time since you have thought numerically so brain gym is used to clear the cobwebs. To do this you will need something, for instance a piece of paper, to cover up the answers as you go. Read each question and decide on the answer before checking. When you see a line, you will know to stop your piece of paper at that moment. Don't make notes as the purpose of this exercise is to get you thinking for yourself.

Column 1	Column 2
Start: You are at a car boot sale and have a number of items for sale. You have £20 change in various denominations. (Go to the box below)	You have £39.15. A familiar customer approaches you and reminds you that she owes you £10.99. How much do you have in total?
You sell your sister's old Barbie doll for £1.15. 21.15 How much do you have in total?	You have £50.14. ✗ ~~52.~~ You sell five books at £1.20 each. 50,14 How much do you have in total? 13
You have £21.15, You sell a very old computer for £14. How much do you have in total? 35.15	You have £56.14. 56 14 9 You sell an antique bellow for £11.95. 67 How much do you have in total? ~~68~~ 9
You have £35.15. 39.13 You sell two books for £2 each. How much do you have in total?	You have £68.09. 100- You sell a delft blue wall tile for £31.91. ~~10~~ How much do you have in total?
(Go to the top of column 2)	You have £100. ✗ Of this, how much is profit?
	You made a profit of £80. ✗

Don't worry if some aspects of this were taxing: the more you do, the easier it will become and the quicker you will get. Now let's consider the topic of subtraction.

4.2 Subtraction

Subtraction means taking a number from another number to arrive at a total. The sign for subtraction is −, which is also referred to as the minus sign. Language used to indicate subtraction varies. You may come across:

x subtract y; x minus y; x take away y; the difference between x and y.

Unlike addition, where you can add as many numbers as you like in one sum, when subtracting you work with only two numbers at a time.

In its most simple form subtraction is represented as:

2 − 1 = 1

As with addition, there is a standard method for dealing with subtraction.

For example:

248 − 144

Again, the numbers are separated into hundreds (H), tens (T) and units (U).

	H	T	U
	2	4	8
−	1	4	4
	1	0	4

Explanation:

Starting from the right, with the units column:

8 minus 4 equals 4.

Then the tens:

4 minus 4 is 0.

And the hundreds:

2 minus 1 is 1.

The answer to the sum 248 − 144 is therefore 104.

Now consider the following, a more complex sum:

350 − 191

	H	T	U
	3	5	0
−	1	9	1

Explanation:

At first glance, starting again with the units column, the sum is impossible because you cannot take 1 from 0. To do this it is necessary to 'borrow' from the tens column.

H	T	U
3	⁴5	¹0
− 1	9	1
		9

One from the tens column is borrowed, which means moving that one to the units column, in front of the 0, which now becomes 10. The figure 5 in the tens column is crossed out so as not to lead to confusion and it is replaced with the figure 4.

H	T	U
²3	¹⁴5̶	¹0
− 1	9	1
	5	9

The next part of this sum also presents a problem as it is impossible to take 9 from 4. To get around this, a one from the hundreds column is borrowed, so the 3 becomes a 2. The borrowed 1 is placed next to the 4 in the tens column, providing a figure of 14. Now you can take away the 9: 14 minus 9 equals 5.

Lastly, the hundreds column. The sum requires 2 minus 1 which is achievable, leaving 1.

H	T	U
²3̶	¹⁴5̶	¹0
− 1	9	1
1	5	9

The answer to the sum 350 − 191 is therefore 159.

Even more complex is when you cannot borrow from the column immediately to the left, when this is a 0. For example:

602 − 54

H	T	U
⁵6̶	⁹0̶	¹2
−	5	4
5	4	8

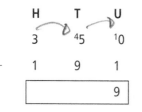

$$n.b) \quad 2.000 - 1.853 = 0.147$$

$$602 - 54 = 548$$

Explanation:

As always, start from the right with the units column: 2 minus 4 you cannot do, it therefore requires borrowing. The tens column cannot help as there are no tens. So you need to borrow one from the column to the left again, that is the hundreds column. The 6 is crossed out, as it now becomes a 5. A 1 moves to the tens column (in front of the 0, to become 10) but as you immediately 'lend' to the units column, the 10 becomes a 9; the borrowed 1 from the tens column moves in front of the 2 in the units column, to become 12. Now you can subtract 4 from 12, giving you 8. Moving to the tens column: take away 5 from 9, giving you 4. There is nothing to subtract from the hundreds column, so this remains a 5.

The answer to the sum 602 − 54 is therefore 548.

If you have more than two sets of numbers to subtract then it is suggested that you take each part separately. For example:

599 − 434 − 45 = ?

First take 434 from 599

599		165
− 434	Then take 45 from the remaining 165	− 45
165		**120**

When you deal with decimal numbers, remember that the decimal point must not move. The numbers are classified as before: hundreds, tens, units, but with the addition of tenths, hundredths and so on. The principle of borrowing remains the same: you can borrow from the column to the left, should this be necessary. For example:

119.90 − 27.88

H	T	U	.	Th	Hth
1	^{1}1	9	.	^{8}9	^{1}0
	2	7	.	8	8
	9	2	.	0	2

TASK 5

Try these:

1.	2.	3.	4.	5.
0.3	4.004	4.834	134.25	5000.0001
− 0.2	− 1.004	− 2.834	− 34.25	− 400.0002
		− 1.853	− 4.25	− 30.0009
			− 0.50	− 2.0003

78

4.3 Multiplication

Multiplication is a mathematical process that specifies how many times a number is added to itself. The sign for multiplication is ×, which is referred to as the multiplication or times sign. The word 'times' is used because you add a number to itself a number of times. An example of multiplication is:

2 × 3 = 6

The numbers mean that if you have three of something twice, then you have six of something in total. It is a way of adding up groups of things quickly without having to add them all up individually. For example, a farmer is selling sheep at a market. Five sheep are placed into each holding pen. There are five holding pens. You could walk around the pens and count the sheep individually. Alternatively, you can use a short cut – multiplication. You know that there are five pens containing five sheep. Mathematically this can be shown as 5 × 5. If you have five lots of five sheep, you have 25 sheep in total: 5 × 5 = 25.

The system for multiplication is as follows:

32 × 65 = ?

The numbers are placed in rows of units and tens, much like adding and subtracting. It doesn't matter which goes at the top as it is the same either way around (it's usually easier to put the higher number at the top).

You first deal with the units; you ask what is 2 times 5. The answer is 10, which is written like this:

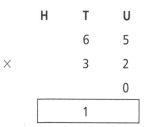

The 0 belongs in the units column; the one is a ten and is placed in the tens column. Next, work out 2 times 6. The answer is 12, plus the one placed below, which makes 13. Record the 3 in the tens column, and the one in the hundreds column.

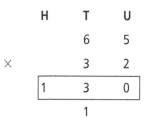

Next you deal with the tens: a 0 is placed in the units column (there are no units to consider here).

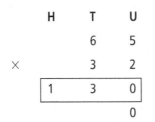

Three fives are 15. Record the 5 in the tens column, and put the 1 in the hundreds column.

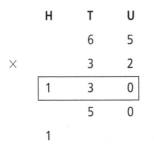

Three sixes are 18; adding the one from the previous calculation makes 19.

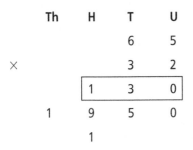

Finally, add the results of multiplying the units and the tens together:

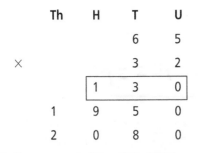

So the answer to 32 × 65 is 2080.

If you are multiplying numbers where hundreds are involved, e.g. 356 × 367, you need to place two zeros before your hundreds calculations because there are no units or tens. For example:

HTh	TTh	Th	H	T	U
			3	5	6
×			3	6	7
		2	4	9	2
	2	1	3	6	0
1	0	6	8	0	0
1	3	0	6	5	2

When working multiplication sums out, there are some short cuts, for instance:

- multiplying by 4: double, then double again;
- multiplying by 5: multiply by ten, then halve the number;
- multiplying by 10: add a zero or move the decimal point one place to the right.

It really helps if you know your times tables, but some people find this difficult, especially the 6, 7, 8, and 9 times tables. If you are one of these people, there are some tricks in which you can use your fingers (or digits) to do multiplication: we call this digimaths.

Digimaths

Referring to the hands below, number your fingers; thumbs are considered fingers.

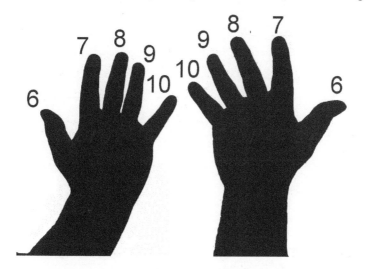

Let's say that you are trying to work out seven times eight (7 × 8 = ?). Take the left-hand finger 7 and make a bridge by touching the right hand finger 8.

To work out the tens count the number of fingers over and including the bridge, (all those fingers above the line). Here there are a total of five, so the answer is fifty-something. To work out the units, look at the fingers under the bridge. Here there are three and two. Three times two are six. The answer is 56.

Digimaths has its limitations, for example 6 × 6 is difficult to calculate. However, it provides a useful alternative to learning all tables by heart.

TASK 6

Complete these multiplication sums:

1.	2.	3.	4.	5.
37	259	3567	555	9876
× 42	× 356	× 68	× 666	× 3456

Handwritten answers: 1554   92204   242556   369630   34~~082456~~   34131456

4.4 Division

Division is a mathematical process that specifies how many times a number is divided or shared by a certain number. The sign for division is ÷.

You can also thing of division as repeated subtraction. How many times can 5 be subtracted from 45? The answer is 9 times, with no numbers remaining. There are two types of division: short division and long division.

Short division

An example of short division is 'What is 48 divided by 4?' Alternatively you can ask 'How many times does 4 go into 48?' The division question is written like this:

48 ÷ 4

However, to work the sum out, we write it as below:

4) 48

This gives you the space for the numbers and your working out:

```
     12
4 ) 48
```

Explanation:

Unlike adding, subtraction and multiplication, where you work from the right, starting with the units, in division you work from the left. In this example the tens are dealt with first. Ask how many times can 4 go into 4? The answer is once, so a number 1 is placed above the 4. The units are next: how many times can 4 go into 8? The answer is two. The 2 is placed above the 8. Therefore, 48 divided by 4 equals 12. In other words, 4 goes into 48, 12 times.

Remainders

Sometimes a number can be divided but there may be some left over e.g.:

5 ÷ 4. Four will go into 5 once, with 1 remaining. This is called the remainder. For example:

57 divided by 4

$57 \div 4 = 14 \, r \, 1$
17

```
     14r1
4 ) 5₁7
```

Explanation:

4 goes into 5 once but there is a remainder of 1. That 1 is placed next to the 7 which becomes 17. Four goes into 17, 4 times but there is a remainder of 1. As you can see this is shown as r1. However many numbers you are dealing with, the principles remain the same.

Decimal divisions

When you deal with divisions containing a decimal point, for example when dividing sums of money, it is essential to ensure that the decimal points remain in the correct place. Neatness and accuracy are the keys. For example:

£136.00 divided by 6

```
       22.66
6 ) 13₁6.4₀4₀
```

Answer: £22.67

Explanation:

6 will not go into 1 so the first two numbers are considered: 13. Six goes into 13 twice remainder 1. Six goes into 16 twice remainder 4. Six goes into 40 six times remainder 4. 6 goes into 40 six times remainder 4 again. Because this is a sum of money, you need to give your answer to two decimal places, so you should find the value of the third decimal place: 6 goes into 40 six times remainder 4 again. The value of the third decimal place is 6, so round up to £22.67 (if the number in the decimal place after the one you need to round is 5 or more, round up; if it is less than 5, round down). Make sure you put the decimal points directly above each other to avoid confusion.

TASK 7

Complete these short division sums:

1.	2.	3.	4.
$5 \div 4$	$15 \div 8$	$135 \div 3 = 45$	$202 \div 5 = 4$
1 r 1	1 r 7	1 5	0 2

(handwritten note: 4 goes 2 into 2 zero!!)

5.	6.	7.	8.
$£500 \div 4 = 125$	$£57 \div 3 = 19$	$£2,000 \div 7 = 2,85$	$£599 \div 8 = 74$
10	2 7	60	39
20		40	3
		5	?

Long division

When the number you wish to divide by has two or more digits, use a slightly different system, referred to as long division.

$$\begin{array}{r} 2 \\ 12\overline{)3343} \\ 24 \\ \hline 9 \end{array}$$

12 into 3 does not go.

12 into 33 goes twice.

Place the 2 above the bar.

$2 \times 12 = 24$

Write 24 under the 33, then subtract: 33 minus 24 is 9.

```
      27
12)3343
      2
      94
      84
      10
```

The 4 is now dropped down next to the 9.

12 into 94 goes 7 times.

Place the 7 above the bar, next to the 2.

$7 \times 12 = 84$

Write 84 under the 94.

94 minus 84 is 10

```
        10
20)202
    20
    02
      0
```

```
     278
12)3343
      2
      94
      84
     103
      96
       7
```

The 3 drops down next to the 10.

12 into 103 goes 8 times.

Place the 8 above the bar, next to the 7.

$8 \times 12 = 96$

103 − 96 is 7

The final answer is 278 r7

(handwritten notes in Italian): zero, ma se il num è già grande abbastanza, lo zero nn serve

(h.b.) x 2nd aventi netti

TASK 8

Complete these long division sums:

1.	2.	3.	4.
554 ÷ 45	159 ÷ 11	135 ÷ 12	202 ÷ 20
12 r 14	14 r 5	11 r 3	10 r 2

5.	6.	7.	8.
£727 ÷ 21	£579 ÷ 15	£2,000 ÷ 17	£599 ÷ 17

```
        12
45)554
    45
    104
     90
      14
```

```
        14
11)159
    11
     49
     44
      5
```

```
        11
12)135
    12
     15
     12
      3
```

4.5 Averages

There are different types of averages; however, the one most commonly used, and explained here, is the 'mean' average. The mean is calculated by adding up the numbers in a sample and dividing that answer by the sample size. It is best described in an example: a restaurant has an offer for a free ice cream for every customer who brings along a token printed out from their website. The head office is trying to establish how many ice creams per day are given out on average.

Monday	Tuesday	Wednesday	Thursday	Friday
50	37	45	60	108

To find the (mean) average you add up all the ice creams given out, then divide the total by the number of days:

Monday to Friday = 300 ice-creams

300 ÷ 5 = 60

60 ice-creams were given out, **on average**, per day.

TASK 9

Work out the following (mean) averages:

1. The following figures represent the daily takings at the miniature village in the second week of August. How much per day was made during that week on average?

Monday	Tuesday	Wednesday	Thursday	Friday
£185	£200	£355	£250	£400

Answer _1290÷5 1390:5=278_

2. The following figures relate to the number of birds entering the rescue centre. How many have entered per day on average?

Mon	Tue	Wed	Thurs	Fri	Sat	Sun
3	12	8	0	5	14	14

Answer _56 ÷7 =8_

3. The figures show entry numbers for the Hampton Court ice rink in the first week in December. On average what was the daily total between 1 and 7 December?

1.12	2.12	3.12	4.12	5.12	6.12	7.12
Mon	Tue	Wed	Thurs	Fri	Sat	Sun
296	264	322	289	451	623	695

Answer _98.84 2940:7=420_

TASK 9 continued

4. On average what was the total for attendance during the weekdays between 8 and 12 December?

8.12	9.12	10.12	11.12	12.12	13.12	14.12
Mon	Tue	Wed	Thurs	Fri	Sat	Sun
294	278	344	333	421	633	657

Answer ~~69704~~ 1670:5 =334

5. On average what was the total for attendance per day during the <u>weekends in December</u>?

1.12	2.12	3.12	4.12	5.12	6.12	7.12
Mon	Tue	Wed	Thurs	Fri	Sat	Sun
296	264	322	289	451	623	695

8.12	9.12	10.12	11.12	12.12	13.12	14.12
Mon	Tue	Wed	Thurs	Fri	Sat	Sun
294	278	344	333	421	633	657

15.12	16.12	17.12	18.12	19.12	20.12	21.12
Mon	Tue	Wed	Thurs	Fri	Sat	Sun
301	288	349	325	480	673	700

22.12	23.12	24.12	25.12	26.12	27.12	28.12
Mon	Tue	Wed	Thurs	Fri	Sat	Sun
314	254	325	0	0	670	701

29.12	30.12	31.12
Mon	Tue	Wed
241	254	212

Answer ~~8182~~ 8 5352:0 =669

4.6 Percentages

'Per cent' means 'per hundred'. Writing a number as a percentage is a way of expressing it as a fraction of 100. The per cent sign is %.

Calculating percentages

The rules differ for particular tasks and you need to know how to work out percentages using decimals or fractions. Both are considered. First, take a look at the table below, which identifies some percentages and their equivalent decimals:

Percentage	Decimal
10%	0.1
20%	0.2
25%	0.25
50%	0.50
75%	0.75

Percentages with decimals

Example 1

An MP3 player costs £60, but is reduced by 20%. How much do you have to pay?

The rule is to swap the percentage for a decimal then **multiply** the original price by the decimal to work out the discount. 20% is equivalent to 0.2.

$60 \times 0.2 = 12$, so you save £12, paying $60 - 12 = £48$.

Example 2

You want an item of jewellery for £145 but then have to pay VAT on top (17.5%). How much will you pay in total?

17.5% is equal to 0.175. Swap the percentage for the decimal. Next you **multiply** the figure by the decimal: 145×0.175 which is 25.375. The VAT is £25.38 (round up to the nearest penny). Therefore, you pay a total of £145 + £25.38 = £170.38.

Example 3

You go away and think about the jewellery. During this time the VAT goes down to 15%. You decide to buy the jewellery after all. How much will you pay now?

$£145 \times 0.15 = £21.75$

$£145 + £21.75 = £166.75$

Percentages can be used to make comparisons easier where the numbers are unequal. For instance, you have scored 41 marks out of a possible 50 in an exam. In another exam you scored 53 marks out of a possible 62. To give you an idea of in which exam you scored better, it is easier to compare using percentages.

Example 4

When working out the result of an exam as a percentage, you have two numbers: the total marks possible and the marks scored by you. In the example above you have scored 41 out of a possible 50 in the first exam.

The rule is: **divide** the small number (the score) by the big one (the total possible), then multiply by 100. At first sight that does seem a peculiar thing to do as normally you divide big numbers by smaller ones, as in the division exercises. This helps you remember the rule:

Small ÷ **Big** × 100

To write the first exam result as a percentage you divide 41 by 50, then multiply by 100:

$41 \div 50 = 0.82$

$0.82 \times 100 = 82\%$

(handwritten: ? cm fare divisore con num + pi certo all'inizio ?)

The second exam result expressed as a %:

$53 \div 62 = 0.8548\ldots$

$0.8548 \times 100 = 85.48\ldots$

The first exam result, written as a percentage, is a whole number, so you want the second exam result to have one decimal place, so round your answer to 85.5%. (In fact, a whole number would be all right in this case, but usually one extra place is best: for example, 82.48 would round to 82%, so it would appear the results for both exams were the same, when actually the second result was slightly better.)

Now it is easier to compare the results: you did better in the second exam.

Percentages with fractions

You can also use percentages to find a number, e.g. when you are told there is 25% discount. It is useful to compare percentages with fractions.

Percentage	Fraction
10% ⟶	1⁄10
20% ⟶	1⁄5
25% ⟶	1⁄4
50% ⟶	1⁄2
75% ⟶	3⁄4

Example 5

The MP3 player in example 1, which cost £60, is now being sold with a 25% discount. What do you have to pay?

You need to change 25% into a fraction. Referring to the table above, you can see that 25% is equal to ¼.

So you are looking for ¼ of £60. To find this, divide £60 by 4.

$$£60 ÷ 4 = 15$$

25% of £60 is £15. To work out how much you pay take £15 from £60 which is £45.

Example 6

You are saving up for a holiday and you decide that you can afford to save 10% of your wages per week. You get paid £230 per week. How much will you save each week?

Looking at the chart, 10% is the same as ⅒. Therefore you divide £230 by 10. So you will save £23 per week.

Short cuts

Many people use short cuts to work out percentages: the chart below will help you to recognise the similarities between decimals, percentages and fractions:

Decimal	Percentage	Fraction
0.1	10% ⟶	⅒
0.2	20% ⟶	⅕
0.25	25% ⟶	¼
0.50	50% ⟶	½
0.75	75% ⟶	¾

Finding 5%   Divide by 10 then halve it. Dividing by 10 is the same as finding a tenth, which is 10%. Half of 10% is 5%.

e.g. To find 5% of £44.

$$£44 ÷ 10 = £4.40$$

$$£4.40 ÷ 2 = £2.20$$

Finding 20%   Divide by 10 then double it. Dividing by 10 gives you a tenth, which is 10%. Doubling 10% gives you 20%.

e.g. To find 20% of £55.

$$£55 ÷ 10 = £5.50$$

$$£5.50 × 2 = £11$$

Finding 75%   Halve the number and then halve it again. Add the two results together. Half is 50%, and half of that is 25%. Adding them together gives you 50% + 25% = 75%.

> e.g. To find 75% of £12.
>
> £12 ÷ 2 = £6
>
> £6 ÷ 2 = £3
>
> £6 + £3 = £9

TASK 10

$\frac{8+}{10} =$ $\frac{25 \times}{6}$

$\frac{15 \times}{6}$ $\times 50$

60

```
                        Menu

Starter          . . . . . . . . . £5
Main Course      . . . . . . . . . £10
Dessert          . . . . . . . . . £3

A service charge of 10% will be added to each bill.
```

10% → 0.1

1. A couple have a main course and a dessert each. How much do they pay for the service?

    Answer 10·13 = 13 × 2 = 26 $\frac{26 \times}{0.1}$ = 2.6 $\frac{26+}{26}$

2. A family attend the restaurant; there are two adults and four children. They all have a starter and main course. How much do they pay for the service?

    Answer ~~60×0.1=6~~   90 × 0.1 = 9   10% → 0.1

3. Three youths have a starter and dessert. How much do they pay for the service?

    Answer 24 × 0,1 = 2.4

4. A mother and two children visit the restaurant. The mother has a main course only and one of the children has a starter and main course, the other a main course and dessert. How much do they pay for the service?

    Answer 38 × 0.1 = 3.8

5. You go to the sports shop and see a pair of sport shoes advertised as being reduced by 40%. The original price was £82. How much will you pay?   40 → 0.4

    Answer 82 × 0.4 = 32.8   82 − 32.80 = 49.20

6. You see the food in your local supermarket is near its sell-by date. A large cake was £5. All food is reduced by 75%. How much will you pay for the cake?

    Answer 3,75   5 − 3.75 = 1.25   0.75

TASK 10 continued

7. You are searching the internet, and find a site that is offering all electrical goods at a discount. You are offered a fridge for £297, reduced from £330. By how much, as a percentage, has it been reduced?

    $330 - 297 = 33$

    Answer _____ $33 \div 330 = 0.1$ $0.1 \times 100 =$

8. You pass a test. You got 56 out of a possible 70. What is this as a percentage? 10%

    Answer _____

9. You get the results of another test, which you also pass. The pass mark was 40. You got 45. The test was out of 50. What was your mark as a percentage?

    Answer _____

10. Your friend was not so lucky and failed the test by two per cent. The test was out of 150, and the pass mark was 100. Your friend does not wish to discuss the mark with you. What is the lowest possible percentage to pass?

    Answer _____

4.7 Fractions

Fractions represent a part of a whole. In the diagram below the box on the left is considered the whole, and the boxes next to this represent two halves of the box, each of them is shown mathematically as ½. Individually they are one part of two. If the box is divided into three, you have thirds (⅓); dividing it into four gives quarters (¼).

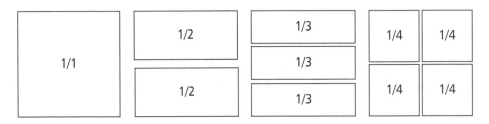

1   A fraction is made up of two pieces of information.

2   The top number is referred to as the numerator. This tells you how many parts you have. The bottom number is the denominator; it tells you the value of the faction.

Adding and subtracting fractions

Adding fractions with the same denominator is straightforward:

$$\frac{1}{3} + \frac{1}{3} = \frac{2}{3}$$

Notice that only the numerator is added; the denominator remains untouched. In a way it should be thought of more as a name than a number. Consider the following sum:

$$\frac{2}{4} + \frac{3}{4} = \frac{5}{4} = 1\frac{1}{4}$$

Where the numerator is greater that the denominator, you calculate how many whole numbers are contained within it. Here, we are dealing with quarters, (¼); four quarters make one whole so the fraction is written not as ⁵⁄₄ but as 1 and ¼.

Subtracting fractions is also a simple process:

$$\frac{2}{3} - \frac{1}{3} = \frac{1}{3}$$

As with addition, you only manipulate the numerator when the denominators are the same value.

Differing denominators

If the denominators are of differing values then you are required to find what is referred to as the 'lowest common denominator' before manipulating the numerators.

$$\frac{4}{8} + \frac{3}{4} =$$

The rule is: whatever you do to the numerator you must do to the denominator. For example the sum is adapted so that both fractions use eighths (⅛).

$$\frac{4}{8} + \frac{6}{8} = \frac{10}{8} = \frac{5}{4} = 1\frac{1}{4}$$

The ¾ has been changed to ⁶⁄₈: both the numerator and the denominator have been doubled. Notice that has been changed to ¹⁰⁄₈: this is because both 10 and 8 can be divided by 2 and is called giving your answer in its simplest form (you could have got the same result by writing the ⅛ in the question as ¾ before adding it to ¾).

If you are presented with two fractions where one is not a multiple of the other, such as ½ and ⅓, you need to find a denominator suitable for both; in this case 6 would be appropriate.

Working out fractions

In order to find out a fraction of a number, for example ⅛ of 24, you divide the number by the denominator the fraction. Here, you divide 24 by 8.

24 ÷ 8 = 3

If five of you enter the national lottery and win a total of £1,500, how much would each person win? In effect you are looking for ⅕ of the amount.

To work this out divide 1,500 by 5.

1,500 ÷ 5 = 300

In both the above examples, the numerator of the fraction was 1, so you didn't need to do anything after dividing by the denominator. If this isn't the case, you can deal with the question in two parts.

If you are looking for ⅔ of a number, first find ⅓, then multiply the result by 2.

For example, to find ⅔ of 48, first find ⅓ of 48.

48 ÷ 3 = 16, so ⅓ of 48 is 16.

Next, multiply 16 by two to find two thirds.

16 × 2 = 32, so ⅔ of 48 is 32,

Consider the following:

Fraction	Divide by	Multiply by
⅗	5	3
⅞	8	7
⁴⁄₁₀	10	4
⁹⁄₁₂	12	9

TASK 11

Complete the following.

1. 3/5 of 20 = $20 \div 5 = 4 \times 3 = 12$

2. 7/8 of 160 = $160 \div 8 = 20 \times 7 = 140$

3. 4/10 of 50 = $50 \div 10 = 5 \times 4 = 20$

4. 9/12 of 144 = $144 \div 12 = 12 \times 9 = 108$

5. $\dfrac{3}{4} + \dfrac{3}{4} =$ $\dfrac{6}{4}$

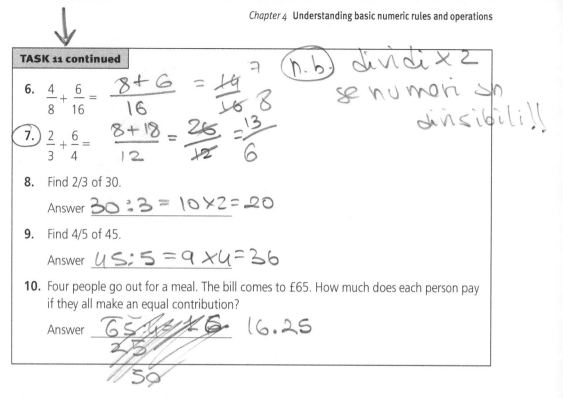

TASK 11 continued

6. $\dfrac{4}{8} + \dfrac{6}{16} = \dfrac{8+6}{16} = \dfrac{14}{16} \to 7 \quad 8$

(n.b.) dividi x 2 se numeri son divisibili!!

7. $\dfrac{2}{3} + \dfrac{6}{4} = \dfrac{8+18}{12} = \dfrac{26}{12} = \dfrac{13}{6}$

8. Find 2/3 of 30.

   Answer $30 : 3 = 10 \times 2 = 20$

9. Find 4/5 of 45.

   Answer $45 : 5 = 9 \times 4 = 36$

10. Four people go out for a meal. The bill comes to £65. How much does each person pay if they all make an equal contribution?

    Answer 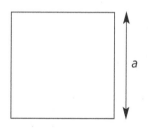 $65 \div 4 \times 6$ 16.25

4.8 Area and perimeter

Calculating the area or perimeter of a shape is an easy process, provided you remember the principles. The principles are explained below; all you have to do is apply what you already know by using addition and multiplication. You will only be required to calculate some basic, two-dimensional shapes, such as squares, rectangles, triangles and circles.

Area and perimeter of a square

Area is *a* squared. a^2

To square a number, multiply it by itself, e.g.

$2 \times 2, 4 \times 4, 5 \times 5$ etc.

Perimeter is the sum of the lengths of all its sides:
$a + a + a + a$ (or: $4 \times a$)

Area and perimeter of a rectangle

Area is length (*l*) times width (*w*)

e.g. $l = 8$cm and $w = 4$cm

$8 \times 4 = \mathbf{32cm^2}$

The perimeter is:

$l + w + l + w = \mathbf{24cm}$

95

Area of a parallelogram

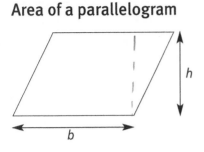

Area is base (*b*) times height (*h*)

e.g. where *b* = 5m and *h* = 5m

$5 \times 5 = 25\text{m}^2$

Notice that the height is the perpendicular height (measured at right angles from the base), not the length of the sloping side.

The perimeter is the sum of its sides.

Area of a triangle

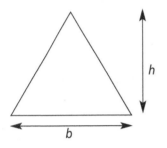

base × altezza diviso 2

Area is ½ base (*b*) times height (*h*)

e.g. where *b* = 8cm and *h* = 8cm

$\frac{1}{2} \times 8 = 4$

$4 \times 8 = \mathbf{32\text{cm}^2}$

Again, notice that the height is the perpendicular height (measured at right angles from the base), not the length of the sloping side.

The perimeter of a triangle is the sum of its sides.

Area and circumference of a circle

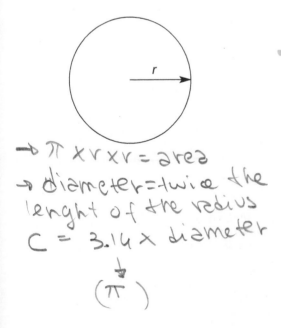

Area is $\pi\, r^2$

π (pi) is 3.141592654 (for general use: 3.14)

e.g. where *r* = 4cm, the area is:

$3.14 \times 4 \times 4 = \mathbf{50.24\text{cm}^2}$

The perimeter of a circle is known as its circumference. The formula for calculating the circumference of a circle is: $C = \pi \times \text{diameter}$

The diameter is twice the length of the radius.

In this example the circumference of the circle is:

$C = 3.14 \times 8 = \mathbf{25.12\text{cm}}$

→ π × r × r = area
→ diameter = twice the lenght of the redius
C = 3.14 × diameter
(π)

4.9 Volume

Whereas area considers two-dimensional shapes, volume considers three dimensions. It is unlikely that you will be asked any more than the very basic shapes, such as a cube or a cylinder.

Volume of a cube

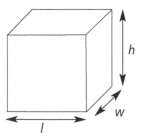

Volume is length × width × height, measured in cubic units.

e.g. l = 3cm, w = 3cm and h = 3cm

$3 \times 3 \times 3 =$ **27cm³**

Volume of a cylinder

Volume of a cylinder is $\pi\, r^2 \times h$

e.g. r = 4cm and h = 12cm

$3.14 \times 4 \times 4 = 50.24$

$50.24 \times 12 =$ **602.88cm³**

*[handwritten: 3 14
16 =
18.84
414
5024]*

[handwritten: moltiplicazioni con punto?]

TASK 12

You have watched some television programmes and want to re-design your garden. You start with some new fencing. The garden measures 20 metres in length and 15 metres in width. You also want some decking. The area for this is 5 metres by 3 metres. Every garden needs a 'water-feature': you decide on a round pond, with a radius of 1.5 metres and a depth of 1 metre.

1. How much fencing do you need? *70 m*
2. What is the area of your decking? *15m²*
3. What is the volume of the pond? *76.5 m³*

[handwritten: 40+30=70]
[handwritten: 15 / 20 / 1.5 / 3 / 5 / 1]
[handwritten: 3·14 × 1.5 × 1.5]

4.10 Time

[handwritten: 3·14 × 1.5 × 1.5]

Dealing numerically with time requires an understanding of the principles of recording time. As you are aware, time is considered in multiples of 60 and 24. For example, there are 60 seconds in a minute and 60 minutes in an hour. Then there are 24 hours in a day.

During the numerical reasoning test you will be tested on your ability to deal with time. If you find it difficult to work out time in your head, there are strategies that you can use, such as drawing the face of a clock with the hands at the times given.

*[handwritten: 76.5 ×
1]*

*[handwritten right margin:
3.14 ×
1.5 =
170
34
51.0
51 ×
1.5 =
255
51
76.5
97]*

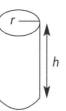

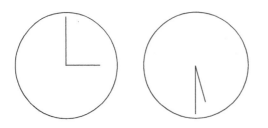

This may make it easier to work out elapsed time.

The above diagram indicates the start time as 3 o'clock and the finish time as half past 5. The time elapsed is two and a half hours. Alternatively you can use boxes of time, where each box represents a number of minutes. In the example below each shaded box represents 15 minutes; the duration of time is shown as two completed hours plus two boxes of fifteen minutes each, making a total of two and a half hours.

	3 o'clock	4 o'clock	5 o'clock
15 minutes	☐	☐	☐
30 minutes	☐	☐	☐
45 minutes	☐	☐	☐
60 minutes	☐	☐	☐

You have to draw the clocks or boxes free hand and have little time to do this. Therefore, don't worry about how untidy it looks; if it helps, it's a worthwhile activity. Further, no one will read your workings out.

TASK 13

The Swan Hotel in Eastshire offers a number of facilities, as detailed below.

Facility	Open	Closed
Restaurant (Breakfast)	6 a.m.	11 a.m.
Restaurant (Lunch)	12 noon	3.30 p.m.
Restaurant (Dinner)	5 p.m.	12 midnight
Bar	12 noon	3 a.m.
Reception	24 hours	
Room Service	6.30 a.m.	12 midnight

How many hours each day are the following available?   5.30

1. The restaurant for breakfast

    A – 3   B – 4   C – 5   D – 7

TASK 13 continued

2. The restaurant for lunch

   A – 3   B – 3.5   C – 4   D – 4.5   5

3. The restaurant for dinner   8.5

   A – 5   B – 6   C – 7   D – 8   7

4. The bar

   A – 17   B – 16   C – 14   D – 15

5. Room service

   A – 17.5   B – 16   C – 16.5   D – 17

6. The restaurant for any meal

   A – 16.5   B – 18   C – 15.5   D – 17

Brain workout 2

Addition and subtraction with time

If you find it assists, use either the clock faces or boxes as detailed above.

It is 4 p.m.

Dinner is in three hours.

What time will this be?   7 p.m.

It's seven o'clock.

Half an hour ago I was working late in the office.

What time was that?   6.30 p.m.   6.30 p.m.

It's half past six.

My train leaves in one and a half hours.

At what time does it leave?   8

It's eight o'clock.

My train journey takes 45 minutes and then I have a 15 minute walk home.   9

What time do I get home?

It's nine o'clock.

Top Gear started forty minutes ago.

What time did it start? 8 . 2 0

It's twenty past eight. 11.30 8.20

I will go to bed in three hours and 10 minutes.

What time will that be? ~~3.40~~ 4.40 . 11.30

It's eleven thirty at night.

I have seven hours' sleep. 6.30

What time will I wake up?

It's six thirty in the morning.

I need three-quarters of an hour to wash, dress and eat breakfast.

What time will I be ready? 7.15

It's quarter past seven. 7.15 7.50

I have to be at work by ten to eight.

How long have I got? 35

You have got 35 minutes. 12. 12.45 1.5

At noon I go to lunch. I should be back by my desk at quarter to one. I am late by 20 minutes.

How many minutes am I away in total? 65 → di re ... i

One hour 5 minutes. op. minuti

It is five past one, and I am in trouble with my boss. 13.05 in

I work until five without a tea break to appease her. ore!!

For how long have I been working this afternoon? S

Three hours and 55 minutes. 5.35 7.10

I arrive home at five thirty-five. I am due to be at my friends at ten past seven.

How long do I have?

One hour and thirty-five minutes.   1 . 35

I sit down and fall asleep. I wake up at eight minutes past seven.

How long do I have to get to my friends?

2 minutes.   7.10   19 7.8   40   40
7 13
711   37
I call to say I am going to be late and agree to be there in forty minutes. The conversation takes three minutes.

What time is it now?   7.11
7.1

Eleven minutes past seven.

I find my mobile phone and I find I missed a call twenty minutes ago.

At what time did I receive the call?   6.51

Nine minutes to seven.

How did that feel? It may feel uncomfortable and tiring. The reason is that you may not be used to thinking in this way. However, the more you do, the easier you will find it.

Chapter 5

Numerical reasoning practice tests

17 min

This chapter contains ten numeric reasoning tests. Each test comprises 25 questions to be completed within 12 minutes. So, as you reach the 6 minute mark, ideally you should be at about question 12.

The tests have some form of theme, which you will not find in the actual test but is used here to make the process a little more entertaining. It will have little bearing on the questions, unlike in the verbal logical reasoning tests. The tests will become more challenging as you progress. Remember that you will be under pressure on the day of the assessment. When you are under stress you can sometimes miss the obvious, for example, 'If you have nine garden fences, how many posts will you require?' The answer is ten. This is because there will always be an extra post at the end of the line. It's simple when you are not being tested; however, in test conditions it is possible to read the question you want to see, rather than the one that is actually in front of you. Remember to RTQ – Read The Question!

NUMERICAL REASONING
PRACTICE TEST 1

1. It is 7.55 a.m. and you are in the local superstore. You spend £18.67 on items for a BBQ. How much change do you get from a £20 note?

   A £0.33   B £3.33   C £1.33   D £2.33   A   B   C   D

2. You go to the butchers and buy the following.

   Sausages   £4
   Burgers   £6.58
   Bread Rolls   £2
   Charcoal   £5
   Matches   £0.50
   How much have you spent in total?

   A £17.08   B £18.88   C £18.08   D £17.88   A   B   C   D

3. Next you go to the superstore where you know they have soft drinks on a special offer: 'Buy two get third free'. If you buy 12 bottles of drink at £1.15 each, how much will you spend in total?

   A £6.20   B £6.90   C £9.20   D £8.20   A   B   C   D

4. You decide to buy some peanuts while you are there. They are sold in packets of 400 grams. If you buy five packets, what is the total weight of peanuts in kilograms?

   A 4kg   B 3kg   C 1kg   D 2kg   A   B   C   D

5. You see some outdoor lights and remember that you need some replacement bulbs. You have three sets of lights. Two bulbs have gone in one set, three in another and just one in the third. In the three sets of lights there are 30 bulbs altogether. How many have broken as a percentage?

   A 20%   B 10%   C 15%   D 40%   A   B   C   D

6. The beer catches your eye. You decide on a relatively cheap beer. The prices are:

   4 cans of Golden Nectar   £2.80
   4 cans of Amber Happiness   £2.90
   4 cans of Macho Largo   £3.20
   4 cans of Richard's Own Ale   £0.90

What is the average price of the beers shown above?

A £1.96   B £2.45   C £2.50   D 9.80   A B C D

7. The more expensive beers don't seem too bad. The prices are:

4 bottles of Super Strength Export	£4.00
4 bottles of IPA	£5.00
4 bottles of Blue King	£4.50
4 bottles of Barentsberg	£6.00
4 bottles of Merry Weather	£6.50

What is the average price of the beers shown above?

A £5.20   B £26.00   C £10.40   D £2.60   A B C D

8. Having chosen your beer, you become distracted by the wine. What to get, is it going to be red or white? The prices of the wines are:

White wine
Green Nunn	£4.50
Pardonnay	£5.00
Peanut Blanc	£6.00

Red wine
Chateauneuf de Curate	£4.50
Psudopetrus	£5.00
Filloux	£4.50

What is the difference in price between the three white and the three red wines?

A £1.00   B £1.50   C £2.00   D £2.50   A B C D

9. You buy three red bottles and three white bottles, just in case. Each bottle contains 75cl. How many litres of wine have you bought in total?

A 3.5 litres   B 4 litres   C 4.5 litres   D 5 litres   A B C D

10. Just as you are about to make your way to the checkout you notice a special offer on the whiskies:

Tutors Whisky	£15	20% off
The Famous Malthouse	£20	15% off
Brown Bush	£25	25% off
Jack Spaniels	£30	50% off

Which of the above is the cheapest following the reduction?

A   Tutors Whisky
B   The Famous Malthouse
C   Brown Bush
D   Jack Spaniels

A   B   C   D

11. After the reductions which whisky is the most expensive?

Tutors Whisky	£15	20% off
The Famous Malthouse	£20	15% off
Brown Bush	£25	25% off
Jack Spaniels	£30	50% off

A   Tutors Whisky
B   The Famous Malthouse
C   Brown Bush
D   Jack Spaniels

A   B   C   D

8 × 5

12. You receive a call from your partner explaining that another four guests will be arriving, making a total of eight including you. You plan to make a fruit drink so buy some oranges. You buy enough oranges for each person to consume five oranges. How many oranges will you buy in total?

A 25   B 30   C 35   D 40   A   B   C   D

13. When you arrive at the fruit section your eagle eye notices a big bag of oranges for sale. The bag contains 200 oranges. How many oranges would each person get if the oranges were split between your guests?   200 : 8 = 25

A 25   B 30   C 35   D 40   A   B   C   D

14. As you enter the bakery aisle you see the baker bringing out fresh rolls. They smell delicious and you can't resist them. If each of your eight guests has three, how many should you buy in total?

A 22   B 23   C 24   D 25   A   B   C   D

15. Finally you are ready to go to the checkout. You pay and leave. You look at your watch: it is 9.05 a.m. You entered the shop at 7.55. For how long have you been in the shop?

A 2h   B 2h 10min   C 1h   D 1h 10min   A   B   C   D

105

16. As you approach your car you notice that the tax disc is just about to expire. It runs out on the 31st of this month; today is the 14th. Including today, how many days are left on the tax disc?

A 17   B 18   C 19   D 20   A B C D

17. As you enter the house you start thinking about how long you have to prepare. The guests arrive at noon. The BBQ takes 45 minutes to heat up to the correct temperature. At what time should you light the BBQ if you wish to start cooking at noon?

A 11.00   B 11.15   C 11.30   D 11.45   A B C D

18. The butcher explained that the sausages would take about 15 minutes to cook, the chicken wings 10 minutes and the burgers 7 minutes. If the sausages go on at midday, at what time should the burgers go on to have the food ready at the same time?

A 12.08   B 12.10   C 12.12   D 12.14   A B C D

19. You have some time on your hands and decide that you will fill up the children's paddling pool with water and ice for the drinks. The pool has a radius of 2 metres and a depth of 1 metre. What volume of water will it take if it is full to the brim?

A 12.56m^3 B 6.28m^3 C 11. 56m^3 D 7.28m^3 A B C D

20. You realise that table space may be an issue for all eight guests. You estimate that each guest should have 0.5m^2 of available table space. Based on this assumption, how much space is required?

A 3.5m^2 B 4.0m^2 C 4.5m^2 D 5.0m^2 A B C D

21. You measure your table. It measures 110cm by 180cm. What is the total area of the table in metres?

A 1.95m^2 B 1.96m^2 C 1.97m^2 D 1.98m^2 A B C D

22. You realise that you need a different table. What measurements should the table be to have a total area of 2m^2?

A 2m $\times$ 2.5m   B 1m $\times$ 3m   C 1m $\times$ 2m   D 1.5m $\times$ 2m   A B C D

23. While you were measuring the tables, the dog has eaten some of the two dozen rolls you left in the kitchen. You are now left with 18, two of which are half eaten, so you throw those away. As a fraction of the total, how many of the rolls have you lost?

A ¾   B ⅓   C ⅔   D ⅜   A B C D

24. Having dealt with the dog and borrowed a table from a neighbour, you see that the time is now 11.45. What is the earliest the BBQ will be ready if the BBQ requires 45 minutes to reach a suitable cooking temperature?

    A 12.15   B 12.30   C 12.45   D 13.00   A   B   C   D

25. The guests arrive, but one couple bring two teenage children who you were not expecting. You have 16 rolls and ten guests. How many is that for each person if they are shared out equally?

    A 1.4   B 1.5   C 1.6   D 1.7   A   B   C   D

13.4 ×
4 =
─────
5.36

NUMERICAL REASONING
PRACTICE TEST 2

1. You return to your car which you parked at the Eastshire multi-storey car park. The cost of parking is no charge for the first hour and then £1.50 per hour, or any part of an hour. Your car was parked for two and a half hours. How much do you need to pay?

   A £4.50   B £1.50   C £3.00   D £2.00   **A   B   C   D**

2. You are just about to drive home when you realise that you forgot to cut some keys, so you return to the shops. It costs £4.25 to cut each key. You have eight that require copying. How much will you pay?

   A £33   B £34   C £35   D £36   **A   B   C   D**

3. You receive a call and are asked to pick up four tins of dog food. You look into the nearest shop and they are charging £0.90 per tin. You decide to go to another shop which you know to be cheaper. Here the tins cost £0.78 per tin. How much have you saved?

   A £0.84   B £0.80   C £0.48   D £0.12   **A   B   C   D**

4. Whilst in the shop you notice a magazine with an article on dog training. It costs £2.99. Combined with the cost of the dog food, how much change will you get from £10?

   A £3.89   B 5.59   C £3.39   D £7.01   **A   B   C   D**

5. It's getting near lunch time and you are feeling peckish. You pass a sandwich shop and buy two rolls and a bottle of water. The water is £0.90; the rolls are usually £1.50 each, but today they have been reduced by 10%. How much do you pay for the rolls?

   A £0.30   B £2.85   C £2.70   D £3.60   **A   B   C   D**

6. You return to the car and see that you need fuel, so you head to the petrol station. Today fuel is £1.11 a litre. Your car's tank has a capacity of 60 litres. If it was completely empty and you filled it with fuel up to the brim, how much would that cost?

   A £66.00   B £66.66   C £111.11   D £66.60   **A   B   C   D**

7. The fuel gauge may be faulty because you have filled the car and it is showing as full when you have put in only 40 litres. What is this when expressed as a fraction of the tank's capacity?

    A ½   B ¾   C ⅓   D ⅔   **A   B   C   D**

8. The petrol pump machine indicates that you owe £44.40. However, you have a Spend and Save card and are due £6.20 off your bill. How much will you pay?

    A £38.20   B £50.60   C £38.24   D £50.64   **A   B   C   D**

9. You look at your watch; the time is 11.35 a.m. You left the house at 9.15 a.m. For how long have you been out of the house?

    A 2h 15   B 2h 20   C 2h 25   D 2h 30   **A   B   C   D**

10. You need to be at a meeting at the local pasta factory at 2 p.m. If the time is 11.35 a.m., how long do you have before that meeting?

    A 2h 15   B 2h 20   C 2h 25   D 2h 30   **A   B   C   D**

11. You receive a phone call: the person you are meeting, Mr Sabatelli, is running late and wants to put the meeting back by half an hour. The time is 11.55, the meeting is now at 2.30 p.m. How much time do you have before the meeting?

    A 2h 20   B 2h 25   C 2h 30   D 2h 35   **A   B   C   D**

12. The time is 11.55; it will take 20 minutes to get home and 30 minutes to get to the location of the meeting. Without considerations of traffic jams or road works, what time should you leave home to arrive 5 minutes before the meeting is due to start?

    A 12.55   B 13.55   C 12.35   D 12.50   **A   B   C   D**

13. You make the meeting on time and, during your discussions, Mr Sabatelli shows you the following sales figures for units of spaghetti:

Mon	Tue	Wed	Thurs	Fri	Sat	Sun
215	304	245	255	301	384	Non working day

    What are the average sales in relation to the working days?

    A 284   B 243   C 264   D 254   **A   B   C   D**

14. You are then shown the sales figures for units of linguini:

Mon	Tue	Wed	Thurs	Fri	Sat	Sun
145	267	145	156	203	266	Non working day

What were the average sales of linguini in relation to the working days?

A 197   B 168   C 189   D 236   **A   B   C   D**

15. You are invited to see the pasta sauce being made. This sauce is sold in 10 litre containers. Each serving of sauce is considered to be 200ml. How many servings are there in each container?

A 50,000   B 5,000   C 500   D 50   **A   B   C   D**

16. You are told that each week the main sauce container is cleaned. This process involves a cleaning agent which is mixed in a ratio of 1 part to 100 parts water. If 200 litres of water are used in the cleaning process, how much agent is used?

A 200 litres   B 20 litre   C 2 litres   D 0.2 litres   **A   B   C   D**

17. The pot in which the sauce is mixed and heated is very large: the height measures 2 metres and the radius measures 3 metres. What is the total volume of the pot?

A $18.84m^3$ B $28.26m^3$ C $56.52m^3$ D $113.04m^3$ **A   B   C   D**

18. What is its circumference?

A 8.48m   B 8.84m   C 18.84m   D 18.48m   **A   B   C   D**

19. In the next room the bucatini is being dried. You notice the large metal-topped tables that are used for the task and are told that they measure 5 metres by 3 metres. There are a total of six tables. What is the total of the area available for drying pasta?

A $15m^2$ B $90m^2$ C $150m^2$ D $900m^2$ **A   B   C   D**

20. You have been told that, when cooked, pasta will increase in size and weight by three times. You are thinking of planning a meal for four people and have been told that 500 grams of pasta will suffice. When cooked, how much will this weigh in grams?

A 1500   B 1000   C 2000   D 2500   **A   B   C   D**

21. You have to get back home to cook. Mrs Sabatelli shares with you the secret ingredient for the recipe for her very special pasta sauce. You need to buy some of the ingredients on the way home:

3 tbsp olive oil	£3.50 for a bottle
3 × 400g cans of chopped tomatoes	£1.80 for 3 cans
tsp dried chilli flakes	£0.99 for a jar
2 tsp balsamic vinegar	£1.72 for a bottle
2 tsp sugar	£0.99 for 1kg

    How much change do you have from a £10 note?

    A £0.90   B £1.00   C £1.10   D £1.20   A   B   C   D

22. You pick up a bottle of wine on special offer, 10% off, normally costing £5. How much discount do you get?

    A £0.10   B £0.25   C £0.50   D £0.90   A   B   C   D

23. Your food cost £9 and your wine £4.50, totalling £13.50. As a fraction how much was spent on wine?

    A ½   B ⅖   C ⅔   D ⅓   A   B   C   D

24. You pour the wine equally into four glasses. The bottle contained 75cl. How much wine is in each glass?

    A 17.25cl   B 20.50cl   C 25.00cl   D 18.75cl   A   B   C   D

25. You put the water on for the pasta and begin to prepare the sauce. You look at the clock and notice that it is 18.15. The dog was last let out at 10.10. How long ago was that?

    A 8h 5min   B 9h 5min   C 8h 0min   D 9h 0min   A   B   C   D

NUMERICAL REASONING PRACTICE TEST 3

1. The laundry service the Best Eastern Hotel in Eastshire charges 50p per item for cleaning socks, vests and handkerchiefs.

    You have three pairs of socks, five vests and four handkerchiefs that require cleaning. How much will this cost you if you use the laundry service?

    A £6.00   B £5.50   C £5.00   D £4.50   **A   B   C   D**

2. The laundry service also dry-cleans clothes. A two-piece suit costs £8.00. How much change will you get from a £20 note?

    A £6.00   B £8.00   C £10.00   D £12.00   **A   B   C   D**

3. The same laundry service charges £1.20 per short-sleeve shirt. You have nine that require washing. How much will you pay for all of your shirts to be cleaned?

    A £9.60   B £11.60   C £9.80   D £10.80   **A   B   C   D**

4. You have four pairs of trousers that require cleaning. The total bill will be £16.

    How much does the hotel charge for cleaning trousers?

    A £2.00   B £4.00   C £3.00   D £5.00   **A   B   C   D**

5. Below are the amounts you spent in the first six months of the year on laundry and dry cleaning at the hotel. On average, how much did you spend each month?

January	February	March	April	May	June
£12	£35.50	£30	£37.50	£45.50	£31.50

    A £32.00   B £34.00   C £32.50   D £34.50   **A   B   C   D**

6. Garments should be handed to reception before 9 a.m. The time now is 7.25 a.m. How long do you have in which to hand in your washing?

    A 1h 25min   B 2h 35min   C 1h 35min   D 2h 25min   **A   B   C   D**

7. The launderette is situated in the hotel. The costs to the hotel on Friday 21 November were:

Electricity	Detergent	Wages	Packaging	Chemicals	Total
£6	£8.20	£80	£2.30	£3.50	£100.00

As a percentage, how much of the costs are spent on wages?

A 88%   B 80%   C 82%   D 84%   **A   B   C   D**

8. The costs to the hotel on Saturday 22 November were:

Electricity	Detergent	Wages	Packaging	Chemicals	Total
£8	£9.00	£80	£3.50	£4.50	£105.00

How much of the costs are spent on things other than wages?

A £23   B £24   C £25   D £26   **A   B   C   D**

9. The washing machines use 50 litres of water per wash. The detergent is mixed at a ratio of 250 millilitres to 10 litres of water. How much detergent would be required for 20 washes?

A 25 litres   B 30 litres   C 35 litres   D 40 litres   **A   B   C   D**

10. The dry-cleaning machine in the hotel has a basket capacity of 10 kilos. Today the total weight of clothes that require cleaning is 50 kilos. How many washes will be required?

A 1   B 10   C 5   D 15   **A   B   C   D**

11. The dry-cleaning process uses a solvent called 'perc' in the trade. The ideal flow rate is 8 litres of solvent per kilogram of garments per minute, depending on the size of the machine. The hotel's dry cleaner holds 10 kilos of garments. How many litres of solvent are required per minute?

A 20 litres   B 40 litres   C 60 litres   D 80 litres   **A   B   C   D**

12. A typical wash cycle lasts for 8–15 minutes, depending on the type of garments and degree of soiling. There are five loads of garments to clean. Discounting loading and unloading times, what is the shortest amount of time it will take for all the garments to be washed?

A 30min   B 40min   C 55min   D 75min   **A   B   C   D**

13. What is the longest amount of time it will take for all the garments to be washed?

A 90min   B 85min   C 80min   D 75min   **A   B   C   D**

14. Modern machines recover about 99.99% of the solvent used in the cleaning process. The hotel's machine is much older and recovers 75% of the solvent. What is this when shown as a fraction?

A ½   B ⅔   C ¾   D ⅘   **A   B   C   D**

15. During the drying cycle, the garments are tumbled in warm air at a temperature of 63°C. The normal working temperature in the launderette is quite warm at 27°C. In centigrade, what is the difference between the two temperatures?

    A 32°C   B 34°C   C 36°C   D 38°C   **A   B   C   D**

16. Mr Wan, the launderette manager, would like a new machine. The machine he would prefer costs about £55,000. If the launderette makes a profit of £5,500 per year, how long will it be before the money is raised to buy a new machine?

    A 10 years   B 1 year   C 11 years   D 100 years   **A   B   C   D**

17. The area in which Mr Wan works is very cramped and shown below.

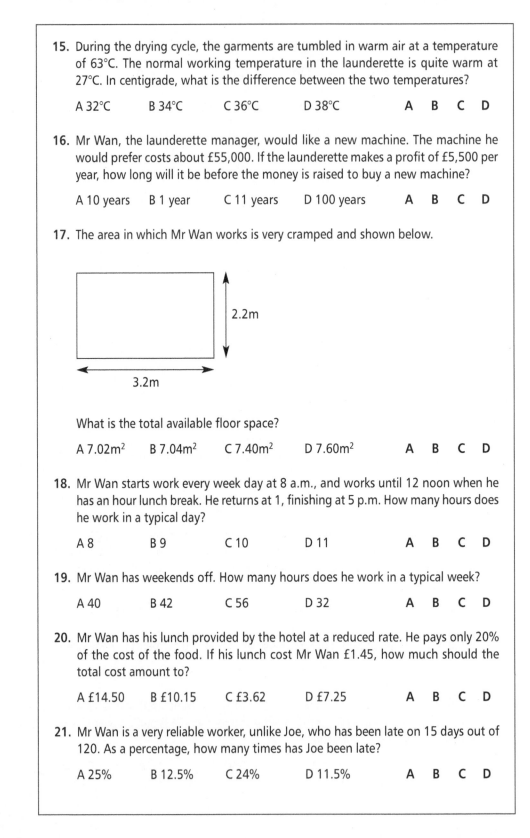

    2.2m

    3.2m

    What is the total available floor space?

    A 7.02m²   B 7.04m²   C 7.40m²   D 7.60m²   **A   B   C   D**

18. Mr Wan starts work every week day at 8 a.m., and works until 12 noon when he has an hour lunch break. He returns at 1, finishing at 5 p.m. How many hours does he work in a typical day?

    A 8   B 9   C 10   D 11   **A   B   C   D**

19. Mr Wan has weekends off. How many hours does he work in a typical week?

    A 40   B 42   C 56   D 32   **A   B   C   D**

20. Mr Wan has his lunch provided by the hotel at a reduced rate. He pays only 20% of the cost of the food. If his lunch cost Mr Wan £1.45, how much should the total cost amount to?

    A £14.50   B £10.15   C £3.62   D £7.25   **A   B   C   D**

21. Mr Wan is a very reliable worker, unlike Joe, who has been late on 15 days out of 120. As a percentage, how many times has Joe been late?

    A 25%   B 12.5%   C 24%   D 11.5%   **A   B   C   D**

22. Mr Wan works with Joe and Paminder. Paminder works 4 hours a day on weekdays and three hours on Saturday and on Sunday. Joe works 50% more hours than Paminder per week. How many hours does Joe work per week?

A 38   B 39   C 40   D 41   **A   B   C   D**

23. Paminder is responsible for buying the detergents and chemicals for the launderette. What percentage of the costs do the detergent and chemicals account for per five-day week? The details are shown below.

Electricity	Detergent	Wages	Packaging	Chemicals	Total
£40	£45.00	£377.50	£17.50	£20.00	£500.00

A 12%   B 1.2%   C 1.3%   D 13%   **A   B   C   D**

24. This week Joe has cleaned 7 suits, 25 trousers and 64 shirts. Which fraction of the total represents the number of shirts Joe has cleaned?

A ¼   B ⅔   C ⅘   D ¾   **A   B   C   D**

25. Paminder is studying the workplace regulations. According to her fact sheet, the recommended minimum space per person is 11 cubic metres.

The diagram shows the dimensions of the laundry workspace.

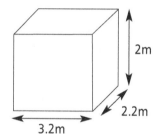

2m

2.2m

3.2m

How many cubic metres are available to all three people?

A 14.08m³   B 15.09m³   C 16.00m³   D 17.01m³   **A   B   C   D**

NUMERICAL REASONING PRACTICE TEST 4

1. You are thinking about going on holiday to New York. The distance is 3471 miles. If you take the return trip, how far will you have travelled?

   A 5842 miles B 6942 miles C 7667 miles D 8456 miles   **A   B   C   D**

2. You are also considering going to Goa. The distance is 4697 miles. If you take the return trip, how far will you have travelled?

   A 9494 miles B 9393 miles C 9493 miles D 9394 miles   **A   B   C   D**

3. You earn £25,600 per year and your partner earns £19,500. What is your combined income?

   A £45,100   B £54,100   C £34,100   D £65,100   **A   B   C   D**

4. You are going to a U2 concert. There are 40,000 people at the concert, paying £50 each. How much money has been made in total ticket sales?

   A £2,000,000   B £2,400,000   C £2,500,000   D £200,000   **A   B   C   D**

5. As well as the 40,000 fans attending the concert, a further 2,700,000 are watching it live on the television and 55,000 are watching on their computer. How many people are watching the concert in total?

   A 2,855,000   B 285,500   C 2,795,000   D 279,500   **A   B   C   D**

6. A couple of days after the concert you are feeling ill. The doctor prescribes some medicine. You are told to take two 5 millilitre doses each day. The bottle contains 100 millilitres. How many days will the medicine last?

   A 5 days   B 10 days   C 20 days   D 50 days   **A   B   C   D**

7. You finish your medicine and feel no better, so you return to the doctor. She is seeing people at an average of 10 minutes per person. You are eighth in the queue. How long will you have to wait?

   A 1h 10min   B 1h   C 1h 20min   D 50min   **A   B   C   D**

8. You take your loose change to the local shop. You have 100 pennies, 50 two-pence pieces, 20 five-pence pieces and 15 fifty-pence pieces. How much do you have in total?

   A £17.50   B £10.50   C £16.50   D £6.50   **A   B   C   D**

9. A group of nine friends win a lottery. The prize totals £405,000. How much will each person be given if it is shared equally?

   A £9,000   B £90,000   C £4,500   D £45,000   **A   B   C   D**

10. It is time to decorate a room. You know that the larger the paint pot, the better the value. You need 16 litres. The paint comes in three sizes: 5 litres, 2 litres and 1 litre. What is the minimum number of tins you need to buy?

    A 3   B 4   C 5   D 6   **A   B   C   D**

11. The painting was such as success that you decide to do another wall. The wall measures 4.5 by 2.3 metres. What is the area?

    A 6.80m²   B 9.15m²   C 10.35m²   D 13.60m²   **A   B   C   D**

12. You are helping someone with their homework. You have been asked to find fractions that are equivalent to a half. In which of the following groups do all the fractions represent ½?

    A $\dfrac{3}{6}$, $\dfrac{5}{7}$, $\dfrac{4}{8}$

    B $\dfrac{7}{14}$, $\dfrac{5}{10}$, $\dfrac{12}{24}$

    C $\dfrac{3}{8}$, $\dfrac{6}{12}$, $\dfrac{7}{8}$

    D $\dfrac{9}{18}$, $\dfrac{8}{16}$, $\dfrac{2}{10}$

    A   B   C   D

13. Which of the following fractions is the largest?

    A $\dfrac{1}{1,000}$ C $\dfrac{3}{100,000}$

    B $\dfrac{2}{10,000}$ D $\dfrac{4}{1,000,000}$

    A   B   C   D

14. There are 36 people at a party, three quarters of whom are women. How many women are there?

A 12   B 27   C 18   D 9   **A   B   C   D**

15. The first course being served is cucumber soup. The recipe consists of three cucumbers, one onion, one leek and 1000ml of vegetable stock. This serves four people. How many cucumbers would be required for eight people?

A 3   B 4   C 5   D 6   **A   B   C   D**

16. How much vegetable stock would be required to serve six people?

A 150ml   B 2000ml   C 1500ml   D 2500ml   **A   B   C   D**

17. What is $\frac{7}{100}$ expressed as a decimal?

A 0.07   B 0.7   C 7   D 70   **A   B   C   D**

18. What is $\frac{7}{100}$ expressed as a percentage?

A 0.07%   B 0.7%   C 7%   D 70%   **A   B   C   D**

19. You are at the sales. Jumpers selling for £80 have been reduced by 25%. How much will you pay now?

A £64   B £72   C £54   D £60   **A   B   C   D**

20. You buy a large bag of potatoes weighing 16kg; 40% is used to make chips for a children's party. How much is this in kg?

A 9.60   B 6.40   C 4.90   D 3.60   **A   B   C   D**

21. You spend lots of money at the supermarket and as a reward they give you a token of 5% off the cost of your petrol. You fill up and the bill comes to £44. How much will your bill be?

A £41.80   B £2.20   C £39.60   D 40.00   **A   B   C   D**

22. You travel to your parents, leaving home at 10.40. You arrive at 11.50. How long did the journey take?

A 1h 10min   B 1h 15min   C 1h 05min   D 1h   **A   B   C   D**

23. The diagram below is representative of the plan of a room. You want to fix coving between the ceiling and the wall all the way round the room. What is the total length of coving you will require?

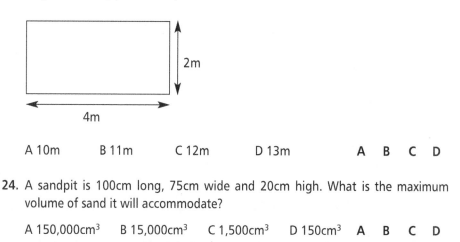

A 10m   B 11m   C 12m   D 13m   **A   B   C   D**

24. A sandpit is 100cm long, 75cm wide and 20cm high. What is the maximum volume of sand it will accommodate?

A 150,000cm^3 B 15,000cm^3 C 1,500cm^3 D 150cm^3 **A   B   C   D**

25. You need to empty the old sandpit, which is 100cm long, 50cm wide and 15cm high. Your bucket has a capacity of 3,000cm^3. How many times will you need to fill your bucket to empty the sand pit?

A 250   B 25   C 500   D 50   **A   B   C   D**

NUMERICAL REASONING PRACTICE TEST 5

1. It takes 248 years for Pluto to travel around the sun. It takes Neptune 165 years. How many more years does it take Pluto to travel around the sun than Neptune?

    A 93   B 83   C 73   D 63   **A   B   C   D**

2. It takes the earth 365 days to travel around the sun. It takes Mercury 88 days to do the same. How many more days does it take the earth to travel around the sun than Mercury?

    A 453   B 737   C 277   D 462   **A   B   C   D**

3. It takes the earth 365 days to travel around the sun. It takes Saturn nearly 30 years to do the same. How many more months does it take Saturn to travel around the sun than the earth?

    A 359   B 336   C 348   D 360   **A   B   C   D**

4. It takes Mars 687 days to travel once around the sun. It takes Venus 225 days to do the same. How many more days does it take Mars to travel around the sun than Venus?

    A 912   B 767   C 519   D 462   **A   B   C   D**

5. If the planet Mercury takes 88 days to travel around the sun, how many days will it take Mercury to travel around the sun five times?

    A 220   B 330   C 440   D 550   **A   B   C   D**

6. It takes Saturn 30 years to travel around the sun. When the earth has travelled around the sun once, what fraction of its journey has Saturn completed?

    A $\frac{1}{30}$ B $\frac{1}{15}$ C $\frac{1}{8}$ D $\frac{1}{60}$ **A   B   C   D**

7. It is roughly 250,000 miles to the moon. It is a little off 10,000 miles to Australia. How many times would you need to complete a return journey to Australia to be the equivalent distance to the moon?

    A 12.5   B 25   C 1,250   D 2,500   **A   B   C   D**

8. You spend £150 on 12 books on Australia. How much on average does each book cost?

A £12   B £12.50   C £6   D £6.50   A B C D

9. ¾ of the 12 books are for other people. What is ¾ of £150?

A £12.50   B £112.50   C £56.25   D £5.60   A B C D

10. You are thinking of taking a trip to New Zealand, and are saving up your money. At the moment you have £600 in the bank, which is receiving an interest rate of 5%. How much will you make on your money in one year?

A £10   B £70   C £60   D £30   A B C D

11. The travel company you are thinking of booking with sells 48,000 holidays each year. Three quarters of these are abroad. How many holidays are abroad?

A 30,000   B 32,000   C 34,000   D 36,000   A B C D

12. Your car breaks down and you are forced to remove £168 from the £600 in your bank account. As a percentage how much has been withdrawn?

A 24%   B 26%   C 28%   D 30%   A B C D

13. The following chart indicates the mileage for your car from January to June.

Jan	Feb	Mar	Apr	May	Jun
320	376	278	355	340	299

During these six months what was the average distance driven?

A 308   B 318   C 328   D 338   A B C D

14. You are working out how much time you spend in your car in a day. Add the following times to give you the total for Monday:

7 hours 40 minutes + 35 minutes + 1 hour 10 minutes

A   8 hours 45 minutes

B   8 hours 55 minutes

C   9 hours 15 minute

D   9 hours 25 minutes

A B C D

15. The following chart indicates the mileage for your car from July to December.

Jul	Aug	Sep	Oct	Nov	Dec
365	868	246	312	345	222

During these six months what was the average distance driven?

A 373   B 383   C 393   D 403   **A   B   C   D**

16. You are working out how much time you spend in your car in a day. Add the following times to give you the total for Tuesday:

1 hours + 40 minutes + 1 hour 45 minutes

A 2 hours 45 minutes

B 3 hours 55 minutes

C 4 hours 10 minutes

D 5 hours 55 minutes

A   B   C   D

17. You are asked to put something into the loft. In order to ensure it will fit you decide to work out the area of the loft hatch, the measurements of which are 1.2m by 85cm. What is the area of the hatch?

A $1.02m^2$ B $1.020cm^2$ C $12.002cm^2$ D $1.20m^2$ **A   B   C   D**

18. You are on the phone, describing the table that you are thinking of placing in your loft. The radius is 70cm. What is the circumference of the table?

A 210cm   B 219.8cm   C 280cm   D 439.6cm   **A   B   C   D**

19. You consider enlarging the loft hatch. You settle for a size of 1.5m by 80cm. If you go ahead with this task, what will the area of the hatch be?

A $1.2m^2$ B $2.1m^2$ C $1.3m^2$ D $2.2m^2$ **A   B   C   D**

20. You have a large chest in the loft measuring 1m by 40cm by 40cm. What is the volume of the chest?

A $16,000cm^3$ B $1600cm^3$ C $0.16m^3$ D $1.6m^3$ **A   B   C   D**

21. Having altered the hatch, you place the table in the loft. It takes you a total of 1¾ hours to complete the job as you have to move some things around to make space. What is the duration in minutes?

A 75   B 85   C 95   D 105   **A   B   C   D**

22. You make your way downstairs and see a delivery of 84 free-range eggs left on the kitchen table. You sell these to friends and neighbours. You have a number of egg cartons that take six eggs each. How many cartons will be required for these eggs?

    A 14   B 15   C 16   D 17   **A   B   C   D**

23. So far this year you have received 504 eggs. You recycled 50% of the egg cartons. How many new ones did you have to buy? (Each carton takes six eggs.)

    A 84   B 42   C 24   D 48   **A   B   C   D**

24. You keep the money you make for the eggs in a jar. In the jar there are 168 $\times$ 1p, 231 $\times$ 2p, 400 $\times$ 5p, 238 $\times$ 10p, 31 $\times$ 20p and 67 $\times$ 50p. How much money do you have in total?

    A £59.80   B £69.80   C £79.80   D £89.80   **A   B   C   D**

25. With the eggs you also deliver potatoes. Each bag weighs 30 kilograms. You have 45 bags: how much do they weigh?

    A 1,350kg   B 2,700kg   C 900kg   D 450kg   **A   B   C   D**

NUMERICAL REASONING PRACTICE TEST 6

1. Using the chart below, calculate the profit for all retailers in 2010.

    Profit for year (£ Millions)

Retailer	2009	2010	2011	2012	Total
1	0.6	1.3	1.4	1.8	
2	0.8	0.2	−0.1	−1.2	
3	2.2	2.6	2.5	2.8	
4	−0.7	−0.8	−0.9	−1.4	
5	3.1	3.5	3.6	3.9	
Total					

    A   £8.4 million

    B   £5.1 million

    C   £6.8 million

    D   £7.7 million

    A   B   C   D

2. Using the same chart, state the total profits for retailer 2 from 2009 to 2012.

    A   −£0.3 million

    B   £1.5 million

    C   −£0.9 million

    D   £1.1 million

    A   B   C   D

3. Using the same chart, state the average profits for retailer 5 for 2009 to 2012.

    A   £3.4 million

    B   £3.5 million

    C   £3.6 million

    D   3.7 million

    A   B   C   D

4. Using the same chart, what is the difference between retailer 1's profits in 2009 and retailer 5's profits in 2012?

   A   £3.3 million

   B   £4.4 million

   C   £2.2 million

   D   £1.1 million

   A   B   C   D

5. Using the same chart, by how much have retailer 1's profits grown between 2011 and 2012?

   A   £0.1 million

   B   £0.2 million

   C   £0.3 million

   D   £0.4 million

   A   B   C   D

6. Using the same chart, on average what are retailer 4's profits from 2009 to 2011?

   A   −£0.6 million

   B   £0.6 million

   C   −£0.8 million

   D   £0.8 million

   A   B   C   D

7. The retailers rely on distribution from the main depot. In total there are 25 retailers around the country. There are 20,275 boxes which need to be distributed equally between each retailer. How many boxes will each one receive?

   A 8.1   B 8,110   C 811   D 81.1   A   B   C   D

8. The 25 retailers were expecting their equal share of 50,000 small boxes. Production has been down at the factory by 25%. How many boxes in total are available?

   A 46,500   B 37,500   C 25,000   D 12,500   A   B   C   D

9. The 25 retailers were expecting their equal share of 125,000 mega boxes. Production has been down at the factory by 50%. How many mega boxes are available to each of the 25 retailers?

   A 2,500   B 25,000   C 10,000   D 1,500   A   B   C   D

10. The fuel capacity of the trucks used to deliver the goods is 50 gallons. There are roughly 4.5 litres to 1 gallon. How many litres do the trucks take?

    A 125   B 50   C 450   D 225   A   B   C   D

11. The cost of fuel per gallon is £4.95. How much will it cost to fill a 50 gallon tank?

    A £49.50   B £495.00   C £24.75   D £247.50   A   B   C   D

12. Truck 1 makes a trip from the depot to retailer 1, a distance of 180 miles. If the truck drove at an average speed of 30mph, how long would it take to get to the retailer?

    A 3 hours   B 4 hours   C 5 hours   D 6 hours   A   B   C   D

13. Truck 2 makes a trip from the depot to retailer 3, a distance of 630 miles. If the truck drove at an average speed of 45mph, how long would it take to get to the retailer?

    A 14 hours   B 12 hours   C 10 hours   D 8 hours   A   B   C   D

14. Truck 3 makes a trip from the depot to retailer 5, a distance of 300 miles. If the truck leaves the depot at 9 a.m. and arrives at retailer 5 at 2 p.m., what is the average speed of the truck?

    A 40mph   B 50mph   C 60mph   D 70mph   A   B   C   D

15. Truck 4 makes a trip from the depot to retailer 2, a distance of 250 miles. The truck leaves the depot at 9 a.m. and arrives at retailer 2 at 2 p.m. What was the average speed of the truck?

    A 40mph   B 50mph   C 60mph   D 70mph   A   B   C   D

16. A female truck driver can consume up to 2000 calories per day. She eats a fried breakfast containing 500 calories. What proportion of the daily recommendation does this represent, as a fraction?

    A ¼   B ⅓   C ½   D ⅔   A   B   C   D

17. A male truck driver can consume up to 2500 calories per day. He eats a fried breakfast containing 500 calories. What proportion of the daily recommendation does this represent, as a percentage?

   A 40%   B 30%   C 25%   D 20%   A   B   C   D

18. The catering for the truck drivers is provided by the company. The idea is to provide the drivers with healthy food. Fresh ingredients are purchased:

   5kg potatoes
   1kg tomatoes
   3kg onions
   2kg peppers

   What is the total weight of the vegetables?

   A 11kg   B 10kg   C 11kg   D 12kg   A   B   C   D

19. The catering department takes delivery of three boxes. The fist box weighs 1 kg, the second box weighs twice that weight, the third twice that of the second. How much do the boxes weigh in total?

   A 10kg   B 9kg   C 8kg   D 7kg   A   B   C   D

20. A tin of beans weighs 440 grams. The catering department have bought 1,000 tins. How much does this weigh in kilos?

   A 400 kilos   B 404 kilos   C 444 kilos   D 440 kilos   A   B   C   D

21. I tonne of cheese has been accidentally ordered; the catering department meant to ask for 10 kilos. How many kilos more cheese did they receive than they wanted?

   A 9.99 kilos   B 99.9 kilos   C 990 kilos   D 90 kilos   A   B   C   D

22. 2 tonnes of potatoes have also been ordered by mistake. Each day the caterers use 25 kilos of potatoes. How long will the order last?

   A 70 days   B 80 days   C 90 days   D 110 days   A   B   C   D

23. A large table in the kitchen measures 4 metres by 1.5 metre. What is its perimeter in centimetres?

   A 11,000cm   B 1,100cm   C 11,110cm   D 1,110cm   A   B   C   D

24. What is the area of the table?

   A 600cm²   B 6m²   C 6,000cm²   D 60m²   A   B   C   D

25. The drivers had a hearty pea soup today. The saucepan has a diameter of 40cm and is 30cm high. What is its volume?

A   15,720cm³

B   150,720cm³

C   3,768cm³

D   37,680cm³

A   B   C   D

NUMERICAL REASONING
PRACTICE TEST 7

1. How is 1.3 billion expressed in full?

   A 1,300,000   B 13,000,000   C 130,000,000   D1,300,000,000   **A   B   C   D**

2. How is 0.25 million expressed in full?

   A 25,000   B 250,000   C 2,500,000   D 250,000,000   **A   B   C   D**

3. In relation to the chart below, in 2009, how many more yachts were moored at pontoon 1 than pontoon 4?

   Number of yachts in Torrevieja harbour

Pontoon	2009	2010	2011	2012	Total
1	28	30	30	30	
2	20	25	30	30	
3	14	16	25	30	
4	5	8	10	25	
5	0	1	9	15	
Total					

   A 22   B 23   C 24   D 25   **A   B   C   D**

4. In relation to the chart above, how many yachts were moored at pontoons 1, 2 and 3 from 2009 to 2012 inclusive?

   A 319   B 318   C 308   D 306   **A   B   C   D**

5. On average how many yachts were moored in 2010?

   A 12   B 14   C 16   D 18   **A   B   C   D**

6. On average how many yachts were moored on pontoon 5 from 2009 to 2012?

   A 6.25   B 7.75   C 8.33   D 9.00   **A   B   C   D**

7. If the maximum capacity of each pontoon is 30 yachts, how full, as a fraction, is pontoon 2 in 2010?

   A ⅚   B ⅝   C ¾   D ⅔   **A   B   C   D**

8. How full, as a fraction, is pontoon 4 in 2011?

   A ⅓   B ⅔   C ¾   D ¼   **A   B   C   D**

9. How full, as a decimal, is pontoon 2 in 2009?

   A 0.26   B 0.37   C 0.48   D 0.67   **A   B   C   D**

10. The equipment for a yacht can be expensive. The *Nimrod* requires some new sheets (ropes). The cost of the rope is shown below. The *Nimrod* requires twenty metres of rope. How much will that be in total?

    Multiplait White Nylon 16mm

Quantity (metres)	Per metre
1–99	£3.05
100–199	£2.81
200+	£2.64

    A £63.00   B £52.80   C £61.00   D £56.20   **A   B   C   D**

11. 5 metres of Galvanised Short Link Chain (6mm) is also required for the anchor at a cost of £4.38 per metre. This does not include the cost of VAT at £17.5%. What is the total cost of the chain?

    A £21.90   B £23.54   C £25.73   D £26.80   **A   B   C   D**

12. The *Dulce Bella* is in need of a traditional compass. The cost of this was £103 but is now £94. As a percentage, how much has it been reduced? Give your answer to one decimal place.

    A 5.6%   B 6.7%   C 7.6%   D 8.7%   **A   B   C   D**

13. The *Stern* is fitted with a new 12 inch brass bell. The bell normally costs £250 but as a loyal customer you get 10% discount. How much do you have to pay?

    A £230   B £247.50   C £220   D £225   **A   B   C   D**

14. The *Orca 3* has torn its mainsail. It is triangular in shape and measures 20 feet in height by 10 feet along the base. What area of material will need to be purchased in order to replace it?

    A 110ft²   B 210ft²   C 200ft²   D 100ft²   **A   B   C   D**

15. The *Lady of the Lowlands* has a new fresh water tank. The measurements of the tank are:

    Length: 85cm
    Width: 35cm
    Height: 22cm

    What is the volume of the tank?

    A 64,550cm³   B 65,450cm³   C 64,460cm³   D 65,460cm³   **A   B   C   D**

16. An alternative water tank measures:

    Length 60cm
    Height 33cm
    Width 33cm

    If two were purchased, what would be the combined volume?

    A 13,068cm³   B 130,680cm³   C 6,534cm³   D 65,340cm³   **A   B   C   D**

17. The *Sowester* requires a new bilge pump. The Grunter model 110 pumps at a rate of 500 litres per hour. How many litres will be pumped in 3 hours?

    A 1,875 litres   B 2,895 litres   C 3,758 litres   D 4,878 litres   **A   B   C   D**

18. There is 6,500 litres of waste to be pumped out of a tank. The Grunter model 88 pumps at a rate of 250 litres per hour. How long will it take to empty the tank?

    A 104h   B 52h   C 26h   D 13h   **A   B   C   D**

19. A spare fuel tank on the *Frosted Orange* is cylindrical in shape. Its radius is 20cm and its height is 15cm. What is the volume of the spare tank?

    A 18,840cm³   B 1,884cm³   C 942cm³   D 94,245cm³   **A   B   C   D**

20. On the quayside some emergency welding is being undertaken. The work started at 8.00 a.m. Each job takes 20 minutes, and there are four jobs. The welder has a tea-break of 10 minutes between the jobs. What time is the work finished?

    A 9.40 a.m.   B 9.50 a.m.   C 10.00 a.m.   D 10.10 a.m.   **A   B   C   D**

21. The *Contrary Mary* is being taken to the workshop to be checked for barnacles. The floor space of the workshop measures 150m by 150m. What is the total area of space available if ¾ of the space is filled with boats?

    A 20, 250m²   B 16,300m²   C 22,500m²   D 16,875m²   **A   B   C   D**

22. A circle needs to be cut into the *Contrary Mary* for extra access. The hole will be replaced by a wooden door. The radius of the circle is 40cm. What area of material will have to be removed?

A 502.4m²   B 1,245m²   C 125.6m²   D 5,024cm²   **A   B   C   D**

23. It will take 16 hours of work to complete the task on the *Contrary Mary*. Due to the fact that some undercoat needs to dry, only four hours will be spent on the boat per day. Today is Wednesday and work is starting today. The boat will be ready immediately following the work. Work will continue over the weekend. When will the boat be ready?

A Saturday   B Sunday   C Monday   D Tuesday   **A   B   C   D**

24. Fibreglass is used with resin and a catalyst. Once the catalyst is mixed in the work must be completed within 17 minutes. If the work starts at midday, what time must the work be finished?

A 13.17   B 13.18   C 14.19   D 12.17   **A   B   C   D**

25. The owners of the *Blue Moon* were promised their boat would be ready on Tuesday at 11.00, but it will not be ready until 13.00 on Thursday of the same week. How many hours late will it be then?

A 48h   B 49h   C 50h   D 51h   **A   B   C   D**

NUMERICAL REASONING
PRACTICE TEST 8

1. You are assisting at the local allotments, helping people grow fruit and vegetables. Your plot measures 20 metres by 20 metres. What is the area of the plot?

    A 200m²   B 300m²   C 400m²   D 500m²   **A   B   C   D**

2. You have a plot to grow potatoes which is triangular in shape. It is 3 metres at the base of the triangle and 3.6 metres in height. What is the area of the potato patch?

    A 10.8m²   B 8.6m²   C 6.2m²   D 5.4m²   **A   B   C   D**

3. You have ordered some turf with which to make instant grass paths. The turf is sold in a uniform size of 1.7m × 0.6m. Your path will measure 25.5m × 0.6m. How many turfs do you require?

    A 17   B 14   C 16   D 15   **A   B   C   D**

4. Your friend hears you are ordering turf and asks you to get five pieces for them. The cost of each piece is £5.15. How much change will you give your friend from £30?

    A £6.25   B £5.75   C £4.25   D £2.15   **A   B   C   D**

5. Another gardener stated that when he ordered turf, the company forgot to quote for VAT and delivery. After he complained, the company agreed to waive the cost of delivery. The cost of the turf was £52.50. How much VAT has to be paid (at 15%)?

    A £7.88   B £8.78   C £7.78   D £8.87   **A   B   C   D**

6. You have a new plot of land that has just been dug over. The soil is poor so you invest in some premium topsoil. The area of your plot is 2m × 8m. You feel that a depth of 20cm will be fine. What is the total volume of the soil?

    A 0.32m³   B 3.2m³   C 32m³   D 322m³   **A   B   C   D**

7. You want to plant some bulbs. A pack of ten tulip bulbs costs £2.69, 12 daffodils cost £3.75 and crocuses cost £4.25 for 30. You buy three packs of tulip bulbs, one of daffodils and one of crocuses. How much do you spend?

   A £16.07   B £13.38   C 16.75   D £13.83   **A   B   C   D**

8. Your colleagues have given you a £50 garden-centre voucher. You spend £35 on bulbs. As a percentage, how much have you spent?

   A 75%   B 70%   C 65%   D 60%   **A   B   C   D**

9. You decide to buy five 80 litre bags of bark. Each bag costs £12.99. You keep two and sell three for £15 each. What is your profit on the three bags?

   A £6.03   B £5.03   C £4.03   D £3.03   **A   B   C   D**

10. There are 100 plots at the allotments. Each plot measures 20 metres by 20 metres. Not counting the paths etc. between the plots, what is the area of the allotments?

    A 400m^2 B 4,000m^2 C 40,000m^2 D 400,000m^2 **A   B   C   D**

11. Someone on the plot next to you drinks on average seven cups of tea day. How many is that in a year?

    A 2,555   B 3,555   C 2,550   D 3,550   **A   B   C   D**

12. You, on the other hand, drink 14 cups of water each day. Compared to your neighbour, what is the ratio of drinks, tea to water?

    A 2:3   B 3:2   C 2:1   D 1:2   **A   B   C   D**

13. Your neighbour loves gladioli. They cost 69 pence each. Using £10 of your voucher, how many can you buy as a present for your neighbour?

    A 13   B 14   C 17   D 15   **A   B   C   D**

14. You both go to the local garden centre where you hunt for the best bargain on fertiliser. You are offered (A) 450g for £4.75; (B) 350g for £3.95; (C) 250g for £2.95; or (D) 150g for £1.95. Which is the best offer?

    A 450g   B 350g   C 250g   D 150g   **A   B   C   D**

15. You find a cold frame, for starting your vegetables, at £499. You pay a deposit of £49. The remainder you pay over a period of six months. How much is each of the six instalments?

    A £75.00   B £83.16   C £90.00   D £64.28   **A   B   C   D**

16. You find a sale where all the clothes are being sold at a third off. You buy a coat which was previously priced as £45, a jumper which was £15 and two tops which were £12 each. How much have you saved?

    A £35   B £28   C £24   D £36   A   B   C   D

17. You visit the grocers where a relative works. She is having difficulty working out her wages. She tells you that this week she worked the following hours.

    Monday   3 hours
    Tuesday   2 hours
    Wednesday   3 hours
    Thursday   1 hours

    How many hours has she worked in total?

    A 8   B 9   C 10   D 11   A   B   C   D

18. In the previous week she worked the following hours.

    Monday   2 hours 20min
    Tuesday   1 hours 40min
    Wednesday   4 hours 40min
    Thursday   2 hours 20min

    She is paid at a rate of £5 per hour. How much is she due?

    A £40   B £45   C £50   D £55   A   B   C   D

19. You make your way to the bank. You take out £30 which is 15% of your savings. How much do you now have in your account?

    A £300   B £230   C £200   D £170   A   B   C   D

20. You go back to the allotment in a cab. The cost is £0.90 per mile and an initial call-out charge of £3. You travel a total of 4.5 miles. How much do you owe?

    A £4.05   B £6.05   C £7.05   D £8.05   A   B   C   D

21. Back at the allotment you take a look at the felt roof on your shed. It needs replacing. The roof is the classic pitched shape, consisting of two identical panels. Each panel measures 1.5m by 3.0m. What is the total area of the shed roof?

    A 4.5m^2 B 9m^2 C 6.5m^2 D 18m^2 A   B   C   D

22. You are given a bag of potatoes. The bag weighs 6kg. There are 30 potatoes in the bag. What is the average weight of each potato?

    A 0.002kg   B 0.02kg   C 0.2kg   D 2kg   A   B   C   D

23. You pick some of your produce: 3.1kg of beans and 1.6kg of strawberries. How many more grams of beans were picked than strawberries?

A 1,500g   B 150g   C 15g   D 1.5g   **A   B   C   D**

24. You have 2.4kg of beans, 3.8kg of potatoes and 1.6kg of capsicum peppers. You use half of each for cooking. What is the total weight of vegetables remaining?

A 3.9kg   B 3.8kg   C 3.7kg   D 3.6kg   **A   B   C   D**

25. You sell 12 capsicum peppers at 45 pence each. The customer pays with a £20 note. What change can they expect?

A £14.60   B £4.60   C £14.20   D £4.20   **A   B   C   D**

NUMERICAL REASONING PRACTICE TEST 9

1   You are at the local Sunday market. There are 100 stalls. You are at stall number one. The stalls are numbered consecutively. How many stalls are there between number one and number five?

   A 5   B 4   C 3   D 2   **A   B   C   D**

2. On average, 700 people visit the market: 500 spend the morning there, 200 the afternoon. If they were spread out equally over the stalls, how many people would be at each stall at 11.00 a.m.?

   A 5   B 4   C 6   D 3   **A   B   C   D**

3. In the afternoon it starts to rain heavily. Normally there would be 200 people, now there are only 50. What is the drop in numbers as a percentage?

   A 100%   B 75%   C 50%   D 25%   **A   B   C   D**

4. The number of stalls has increased steadily over the years. Three years ago there were 50; the following year the number had increased by 20%. How many stalls were there two years ago?

   A 75   B 60   C 65   D 70   **A   B   C   D**

5. You are buying carrots. They are sold for £0.72 per kg. You want 3kg. What will they cost?

   A £2.60   B £1.44   C £2.16   D £2.88   **A   B   C   D**

6. You look elsewhere and find some chantenay carrots at £0.72 per 500g. How much would three kilos cost?

   A £3.50   B £2.88   C £2.16   D £4.32   **A   B   C   D**

7. You see some aubergines at four stalls.

   Stall 1   2 aubergines for £2.36
   Stall 2   3 aubergines for £3.50
   Stall 3   4 aubergines for £4.72
   Stall 4   5 aubergines for £5.90

   Which stall sells aubergines the cheapest?

   A 1   B 2   C 3   D 4   **A   B   C   D**

8. The figures listed below represent the monthly takings for the first six months of the year. On average, how much was taken from January to March inclusive?

Stall 47

Jan   £544
Feb   £1,544
Mar   £1,960
April   £2,332
May   £1,745
June   £2,999

A £1,349.33   B £4,048.00   C £2,024.00   D £134.90   **A   B   C   D**

9. How much was taken from April to June inclusive, after deducting the rent of £100 for each month?

A £6,776   B £6,767   C £7,076   D £7,067   **A   B   C   D**

10. What was the difference between the best and worst months?

A £178.80   B £245.50   C £1,788   D £2,455   **A   B   C   D**

11. Stall 19 made £1,120 last month and paid £280 rent. How is the rent represented as a fraction of the stall's takings?

A ½   B ¼   C ⅔   D ⅜   **A   B   C   D**

12. Stall 49 made £1,400 last month and paid £280 rent. How is the rent represented as a percentage of the stall's takings?

A 50%   B 33%   C 25%   D 20%   **A   B   C   D**

13. You decide to start your own stall. You get up at 4 a.m., arriving at the market at 5.30 a.m. You are allocated a stall at 5.45 a.m. and work until it gets dark at 5.30 p.m. How long ago did you get up?

A 14h   B 13.5h   C 13h   D 12.5h   **A   B   C   D**

14. The following Sunday you get up at 4 a.m., arriving at the market at 5.30 a.m. You are allocated a stall at 6.30 a.m. and work until it gets dark at 5.30 p.m. For how long did you have your stall?

A 11h   B 9.5h   C 8h   D 7.5h   **A   B   C   D**

15. On your stall you sell hot drinks in 250ml mugs. Your hot-water heater contains 50 litres. How many drinks will you provide from one full water heater?

    A 150   B 100   C 250   D 200   **A B C D**

16. Your best seller is your 'Hot Diggedy Dogs! Bonfire Bangers in Wraps'. The sausages come in tins of ten; the wraps come in packets of eight. What is the minimum number of packets of wraps you would need to buy to ensure an exact number with no sausages or wraps left over?

    A 8   B 10   C 5   D 9   **A B C D**

17. For every eight wraps the recipe requires two chopped onions. How many onions will be required for 160 wraps?

    A 10   B 20   C 40   D 80   **A B C D**

18. Your stall measures 2.5m by 2.5m. What is the area of your stall?

    A $6.75m^2$ B $6.50m^2$ C $6.25m^2$ D $6.0m^2$ **A B C D**

19. You place a cover over your stall to keep off the rain. The cover measures 3m by 2.8m. What is perimeter of the cover?

    A 11.6m   B 11.2m   C 12.6m   D 12.2m   **A B C D**

20. It is raining and you have a leak. You have placed an ice-cream container under the leak. The container contains 2 litres. It is filling up at a rate of 20cl per hour. How long will it take to fill up?

    A 20h   B 10h   C 5h   D 2h   **A B C D**

21. You decide to go home and get another cover. A friend takes over the stall and you make the 10 mile journey home. Travelling at an average speed of 20mph, how long will it take there and back (discounting any time spent looking for the cover)?

    A 30min   B 40min   C 50min   D 60min   **A B C D**

22. The spare cover measures 2m × 2m and your stall requires 2.5m × 2.5m. What is the difference in area?

    A $2.55m^2$ B $2.45m^2$ C $2.25m^2$ D $2.15m^2$ **A B C D**

23. A kind person from the market lends you their spare cover. However, it is triangular in shape, with a base of 3m and a height of 3m. What is its area?

    A $2.8m^2$ B $4.5m^2$ C $6.5m^2$ D $9m^2$ **A B C D**

24. You reduce the price of your muffins by 25%. If they are sold at 75p, what was their original price?

A £1.00   B £0.90   C £0.85   D £0.75   **A   B   C   D**

25. Your sports drinks have gone up 25%. The original price was £2.00; what do they cost now?

A £2.50   B £2.35   C £2.25   D £2.15   **A   B   C   D**

NUMERICAL REASONING
PRACTICE TEST 10

1. You are building an extension to your house, which will involve the following miscellaneous costs:

   £1,458.30
   £588.99
   £1,999.95
   £998.99
   _____
   Total _____

   Which of the following matches the total?

   A £5,046.23   B £4,046.23   C £4,064.32   D £5,462.30   **A   B   C   D**

2. You hire a surface scaler. Hire for the first day is £127.50, and any additional days cost £42.60. You guess you need scaler for three days. How much do you have to pay?

   A £225.50   B £221.70   C £127.50   D £212.70   **A   B   C   D**

3. You only need the scaler for two days, but as they fall on a weekend, the weekend rate of £149.10 for both days applies. You pay in cash, allowing you a 10% discount. How much change will you get from £150?

   A £15.81   B £13.78   C £14.45   D £16.98   **A   B   C   D**

4. You are buying bricks to build a wall. There are 60 bricks in one square metre. You buy five square metres of bricks. How many bricks do you have in total?

   A 300   B 400   C 500   D 600   **A   B   C   D**

5. The bricks are 20cm long. The mortar between the bricks is 10mm in thickness. If you lay ten bricks in a straight line, using mortar, how long will the row be in metres?

   A 3.00m   B 2.90m   C 2.09m   D 1.99m   **A   B   C   D**

6. The cost of your bricks is £350 per 1000. Today you buy 6000 bricks. How much change will you get from £2,500?

   A £300   B £400   C £500   D £600   **A   B   C   D**

7. Of your 6000 bricks, you use 4000. What is this expressed as a fraction?

    A ⅔   B ⅖   C ⁴⁄₇   D ⅘   **A   B   C   D**

8. A team of two bricklayers and one labourer lays 600 bricks per day at a cost of £500 per day. How much will it cost to lay 6000 bricks?

    A £3,000   B £4,000   C £5,000   D £6,000   **A   B   C   D**

9. You decide to build a rectangular pond. The dimensions are 2m × 1.5m × 0.6m. What is the volume of the pond?

    A 1.8m³   B 1.2m³   C 2.3m³   D 1.5m³   **A   B   C   D**

10. Your partner prefers a round pond, with a diameter of 2m and a depth of 90cm. What is its volume?

    A 6.28m³   B 2.83m³   C 11.30m³   D 4.83m³   **A   B   C   D**

11. You have purchased the glass for 15 windows. You have been presented with a bill for £3,000. On average, how much did each window cost?

    A £100   B £200   C £300   D £400   **A   B   C   D**

12. VAT is to be paid on top of the £3,000 for the glass. What is the total cost of the glass with the VAT at 15%?

    A £3,150   B £3,300   C £3,450   D £3,600   **A   B   C   D**

13. On average it takes 1 hour to fit each window. There are a total of 15 windows. If all the windows are installed on one day without you taking a break and you begin work at 6.30 a.m., at what time will you finish the task?

    A 8 p.m.   B 8.30 p.m.   C 9 p.m.   D 9.30 p.m.   **A   B   C   D**

14. You order some floorboards and are told that they will arrive on Thursday at 14.50 hrs. It is now Monday at 11.15 hrs. How many hours and minutes will have elapsed when the wood arrives?

    A   80h 15min

    B   51h 40min

    C   75h 35min

    D   72h 25min

    A   B   C   D

15. According to the chart below, the workers are from all over the world. What percentage of the workforce is from Australia?

Country	Workers
Poland	7
India	5
Ireland	10
Romania	8
UK	15
Australia	5
Total	**50**

A 5%   B 10%   C 15%   D 20%   A   B   C   D

16. According to the chart above, UK workers represent what fraction of the workforce?

A 5%   B 10%   C 15%   D 20%   A   B   C   D

17. According to the chart above, what percentage of the workforce is from non-English speaking countries?

A 30%   B 40%   C 50%   D 60%   A   B   C   D

18. You have ordered a number of RSJs (Reinforced Steel Joists). They will have to be lifted in using of a crane. The crane travels 15 miles to get to you and the journey takes 45 minutes. What is the average speed of the crane?

A 25mph   B 15mph   C 20mph   D 10mph   A   B   C   D

19. One of the RSJs weighs 16kg per metre. Its total length is 3.25 metres. How much does it weigh?

A 52kg   B 48kg   C 25kg   D 16kg   A   B   C   D

20. Three RSJs are to be lifted into place; they all weigh 16kg per metre. Their lengths are:

3.5m
4m
4.8m

What is the combined weight of the RSJs?

A 65.6kg   B 157.6kg   C 196.8kg   D 200kg   A   B   C   D

21. As the crane departs, the M24 truck-mounted concrete pump arrives. It can deliver 110m³ of concrete in 1 hour. How long will it take to deliver 357.50m³ of concrete?

    A 2h   B 2h 20min   C 3h   D 3h 15min   **A   B   C   D**

22. The M63 pump delivers concrete at a rate of 160m³ per hour. If the M63 were used, how much would be delivered in 2.5 hours?

    A 600m³   B 430m³   C 320m³   D 400m³   **A   B   C   D**

23. A cylindrical water tank is being used on the site. Its radius is 0.90m and its height is 1.90m. What is total volume of the tank?

    A 4.83m³   B 483m³   C 4,832m³   D 4,832,46m³   **A   B   C   D**

24. The mix of the concrete is:

    1 unit × cement

    2 unit × fine aggregate

    4 unit × coarse aggregate

    If you were to use 12 units of coarse aggregate, how many units of cement would be required?

    A 3   B 4   C 5   D 6   **A   B   C   D**

25. The building work has finished. You have stayed within budget, spending 98% of the total £10,000 set aside. How much money do you have left over?

    A £450   B £300   C £200   D £250   **A   B   C   D**

Epilogue

Reflective practice

Reflecting on what you are doing and how you may do better is a very important aspect of your learning. It enables you to face reality by thinking about how well you have done something and working out a strategy to improve what you are doing on the next occasion.

Roffey-Barentsen and Malthouse (2009, p.6), describe Kolb's (1984) reflective model in everyday language to describe the process. The model can be started at any stage.

The reflective practice model is described as follows.

1. **Do it**   This can be anything from working out a sum to painting the house.

2. **Reflect on it**   You think about what went well, what went less well, what you did, what you didn't do, the reasons for that, etc. For example, you may identify that you do not understand how to do fractions.

3. **Read up on it**   You read a book, search the internet or speak to someone who knows about the subject. In the example given, look up how to do fractions, by looking at mathematics books or the internet, or even enrolling on a numeracy programme.

4. **Plan the next stage**   Now you have decided what you should do differently you can plan the next stage and decide on what it is exactly that you will do differently on the next occasion. In the example, you have read up about fractions; now plan to do some more sums using fractions.

Reflective practice means that you can identify what you need to do, based on the assumption that you are ideally placed to recognise your own strengths and areas for development. Honesty is paramount as a delusional X-Factor type belief in yourself, regardless of obvious inability, is not going to get you anywhere. An honest and frank look at your ability, combined with the willingness to change, are the essential ingredients for your success.

ANSWERS TO THE VERBAL LOGICAL REASONING PRACTICE TESTS

Test 1 → 7 err.

1.	C	9.	C	17.	A	25.	A
2.	B	10.	B	18.	B	26.	A
3.	C	11.	C	19.	C	27.	C
4.	A	12.	C	20.	B	28.	C
5.	C	13.	C	21.	C	29.	C
6.	B	14.	B	22.	C	30.	C
7.	C	15.	A	23.	C	31.	A
8.	A	16.	C	24.	B		

Test 2 → 4 err.

1.	A	9.	C	17.	C	25.	C
2.	B	10.	B	18.	B	26.	B
3.	A	11.	B	19.	A	27.	A
4.	C	12.	A	20.	B	28.	B
5.	C	13.	A	21.	B	29.	A
6.	B	14.	B	22.	B	30.	C
7.	A	15.	B	23.	A	31.	C
8.	B	16.	A	24.	C		

Test 3 → 6 err.

1.	A	9.	B	17.	B	25.	A
2.	B	10.	C	18.	B	26.	B
3.	A	11.	A	19.	C	27.	B
4.	B	12.	B	20.	B	28.	B
5.	B	13.	B	21.	B	29.	A
6.	C	14.	C	22.	C	30.	B
7.	B	15.	B	23.	B	31.	C
8.	B	16.	B	24.	B		

Test 4 → 7 err.

1. B	9. C	17. A	25. A
2. C	10. B	18. C	26. B
3. A	11. A	19. A	27. C
4. B	12. A	20. A	28. C
5. A	13. A	21. C	29. A
6. C	14. B	22. A	30. B
7. A	15. C	23. B	31. B
8. A	16. C	24. A	

Test 5 → 7 err.

1. B	9. B	17. C	25. A
2. B	10. A	18. C	26. B
3. C	11. A	19. A	27. B
4. C	12. B	20. C	28. B
5. B	13. B	21. A	29. B
6. C	14. B	22. C	30. C
7. A	15. B	23. A	31. A
8. A	16. B	24. C	

Test 6 → 7 err.

1. B	9. C	17. B	25. B
2. A	10. A	18. A	26. B
3. B	11. C	19. B	27. A
4. B	12. A	20. A	28. B
5. B	13. A	21. A	29. C
6. B	14. B	22. A	30. C
7. C	15. A	23. B	31. A
8. A	16. C	24. C	

Test 7 → 5 err.

1. A	9. A	17. A	25. C
2. B	10. B	18. B	26. A
3. A	11. C	19. C	27. B
4. A	12. B	20. A	28. A
5. A	13. A	21. A	29. C
6. C	14. A	22. B	30. A
7. A	15. B	23. A	31. B
8. B	16. A	24. B	

Test 8 → 4 err.

1.	A	9.	C	17.	A	25.	B
2.	A	10.	A	18.	A	26.	A
3.	C	11.	B	19.	B	27.	A
4.	B	12.	A	20.	B	28.	A
5.	B	13.	A	21.	A	29.	B
6.	A	14.	B	22.	C	30.	C
7.	B	15.	C	23.	C	31.	B
8.	A	16.	C	24.	A		

Test 9 → 8 err.

1.	B	9.	B	17.	B	25.	B
2.	B	10.	B	18.	A	26.	A
3.	B	11.	B	19.	C	27.	C
4.	C	12.	C	20.	B	28.	C
5.	A	13.	C	21.	A	29.	B
6.	A	14.	B	22.	A	30.	B
7.	A	15.	C	23.	B	31.	B
8.	B	16.	A	24.	C		

Test 10 → 5 err.

1.	A	9.	B	17.	A	25.	A
2.	A	10.	C	18.	C	26.	A
3.	C	11.	B	19.	B	27.	C
4.	A	12.	B	20.	C	28.	A
5.	B	13.	A	21.	B	29.	B
6.	B	14.	A	22.	B	30.	A
7.	A	15.	C	23.	A	31.	B
8.	A	16.	C	24.	A		

ANSWERS TO THE NUMERICAL TASKS

Task 1

49   9 units, 4 tens

274   4 units, 7 tens, 2 hundreds

2211   1 unit, 1 ten, 2 hundreds, 2 thousands

63503   3 units, 0 tens, 5 hundreds, 3 thousands, 6 ten-thousands

271959 9 units, 5 tens, 9 hundreds, 1 thousand, 7 ten-thousands, 2 hundred-thousands

Task 2

1.	2.	3.	4.	5.	6.
23	359	311	1010	39378	929992
+ 48	+ 354	943	101	3398	874674
71	**713**	+ 99	1101	38888	238944
		1353	+ 1011	+ 98988	+ 879266
			3223	**180652**	**2922876**

Task 3

1.	2.	3.	~~4.~~	~~5.~~	~~6.~~
0.3	0.004	2.834	33.25	1000.0001	101099.9
+ 0.2	+ 1.004	2.834	34.25	2000.0002	27.4
0.5	**1.008**	+ 2.854	34.25	1000.0009	454545.0005
		8.522	+ 32.50	+ 1000.0003	+ 1.1
			134.25	**5000.0015**	**555673.4005**

Task 4

1.	2.	3.	~~4.~~	5.
£ 0.55	£ 9.04	£ 15.99	£ 589.50	£ 1,000,000.00
+ £ 0.55	+ £ 1.03	£ 16.99	£ 989.25	£ 2,000,000.00
£ 1.10	**£ 10.07**	+ £ 20.99	£ 978.25	£ 100,000.00
		£ 53.97	+ £ 936.50	+ £ 1,000.00
			£ 3493.50	**£ 3,101,000.00**

Task 5

1.	2.	3.	4.	5.
0.3	4.004	4.834	134.25	5000.0001
− 0.2	− 1.004	− 2.834	− 34.25	− 400.0002
0.1	**3.000**	**2.000**	**100.00**	**4599.9999**
		− 1.853	− 4.25	− 30.0009
		0.147	**95.75**	**4569.999**
			− 0.50	− 2.0003
			95.25	**4567.9987**

Task 6

1.	2.	3.	4.	~~5.~~
37	259	3567	555	9876
− 42	− 356	− 68	− 666	− 3456
74	1554	28536	3330	59256
1480	12950	254020	33300	493800
1554	77700	**242556**	333000	3950400
	92204		**369630**	29628000
				34131456

Task 7

1.	2.	3.	~~4.~~
$5 \div 4 = \mathbf{1\ r1}$	$15 \div 8 = \mathbf{1\ r7}$	$135 \div 3 = \mathbf{45}$	$202 \div 5 = \mathbf{40\ r2}$

5.	6.	~~7.~~	~~8.~~
$£500 \div 4 = \mathbf{£125}$	$£57 \div 3 = \mathbf{£19}$	$£2,000 \div 7 = \mathbf{£285.71}$	$£599 \div 8 = \mathbf{£74.87}$

Task 8

~~1.~~	2.	3.	4.
$554 \div 45 = \mathbf{12\ r4}$	$159 \div 11 = \mathbf{14\ r5}$	$135 \div 12 = \mathbf{11\ r3}$	$202 \div 20 = \mathbf{10\ r2}$

5.	6.	7.
$£727 \div 21 = \mathbf{£24.61}$ (3)	$£579 \div 15 = \mathbf{£38.60}$	$£2,000 \div 17 = \mathbf{£117.64}$

8.

$£599 \div 17 = \mathbf{£35.23}$

Task 9

~~1.~~
```
    185
    200
    355
    250
  + 400
```
$1390 \div 5 = \mathbf{278}$

2.
```
      3
     12
      8
      0
      5
     14
   + 14
```
$56 \div 7 = \mathbf{8}$

3.
```
    296
    264
    322
    289
    451
    623
  + 695
```
$2940 \div 7 = \mathbf{420}$

4. 294
    278
    344
    333
    + 421

    $1670 \div 5 =$ **334**

5. 623
    695
    633
    657
    673
    700
    670
    + 701

    $5352 \div 8 =$ **669**

Task 10

1. £10
    £10
    £3
    £3

    $£26 \times 0.1 =$ **£2.60**

2. Starters $6 \times 5 = £30$
    Main course $6 \times 10 = £60$

    Total $£90 \times 0.1 =$ **£9**

3. Starters $3 \times 5 = £15$
    Desserts $3 \times 3 = £9$

    Total $£24 \times 0.1 =$ **£2.40**

4. Starters $1 \times 5 = £5$
    Main courses $3 \times 10 = £30$
    Desserts $1 \times 3 = £3$

    Total $£38 \times 0.1 =$ **£3.80**

5. $£82 \times 0.4 = £32.80$
        £82.00
    − £32.80
        £49.20

6. $£5 \times 0.75 = £3.75$
        £5.00
    − £3.75
        £1.25

7. £330 − £297 = £33
    33 ÷ 330 = 0.1
    0.1 × 100 = **10%**

8. 56 ÷ 70 = 0.8
    0.8 × 100 = **80%**

9. 45 ÷ 50 = 0.9
    09. × 100 = **90%**

10. 100 ÷ 150 = 0.666. . . giving 0.67 to two decimal places
    0.67 × 100 = **67%**

Task 11

1. 3/5 of 20 = **12**

2. 7/8 of 160 = **140**

3. 4/10 of 50 = **20**

4. 9/12 of 144 = **108**

5. $\dfrac{3}{4} + \dfrac{3}{4} = \dfrac{6}{4} = 1\dfrac{2}{4} = 1\frac{1}{2}$

6. $\dfrac{4}{8} + \dfrac{6}{16} = \dfrac{8}{16} + \dfrac{6}{16} = \dfrac{14}{16} = \dfrac{7}{8}$

7. $\dfrac{2}{3} + \dfrac{6}{4} = \dfrac{8}{12} + \dfrac{18}{12} + \dfrac{26}{12} = 2\frac{1}{6}$

8. 30 ÷ 3 = 10   10 × 2 = **20**

9. 45 ÷ 5 = 9   4 × 9 = **36**

10. £65 ÷ 4 = **£16.25**

Task 12

1. 70m

2. 15m²

3. 7.065m³

Task 13

1. C (5 hours)   4. D (15 hours)

2. B (3.5 hours)   5. A (17.5 hours)

3. C (7 hours)   6. C (15.5 hours)

ANSWERS TO THE NUMERICAL REASONING PRACTICE TESTS

Test 1   6 err.

1.	C	7.	A	13.	A	19.	A
2.	C	8.	B	14.	C	20.	B
3.	C	9.	C	15.	D	21.	D
4.	D	10.	A	16.	B	22.	C
5.	A	11.	C	17.	B	23.	B
6.	B	12.	D	18.	A	24.	B
						25.	C

Test 2

1.	C	7.	D	13.	A	19.	B
2.	B	8.	A	14.	A	20.	A
3.	C	9.	B	15.	D	21.	B
4.	A	10.	C	16.	C	22.	C
5.	C	11.	D	17.	C	23.	D
6.	D	12.	B	18.	C	24.	D
						25.	A

Test 3

1.	A	7.	B	13.	D	19.	A
2.	D	8.	C	14.	C	20.	D
3.	D	9.	A	15.	C	21.	B
4.	B	10.	C	16.	A	22.	B
5.	A	11.	D	17.	B	23.	D
6.	C	12.	B	18.	A	24.	B
						25.	A

Test 4

1.	B	7.	A	13.	A	19.	D
2.	D	8.	B	14.	B	20.	B
3.	A	9.	D	15.	D	21.	A
4.	A	10.	B	16.	C	22.	A
5.	C	11.	C	17.	A	23.	C
6.	B	12.	B	18.	C	24.	A
						25.	B

Test 5

1.	B	7.	A	13.	C	19.	A
2.	C	8.	B	14.	D	20.	C
3.	C	9.	B	15.	C	21.	D
4.	D	10.	D	16.	B	22.	A
5.	C	11.	D	17.	A	23.	B
6.	A	12.	C	18.	D	24.	D
						25.	A

Test 6

1.	C	7.	C	13.	A	19.	A
2.	A	8.	B	14.	C	20.	D
3.	B	9.	A	15.	B	21.	C
4.	A	10.	D	16.	A	22.	B
5.	D	11.	D	17.	D	23.	B
6.	C	12.	D	18.	D	24.	B
						25.	D

Test 7

1.	D	7.	A	13.	D	19.	A
2.	B	8.	A	14.	D	20.	B
3.	B	9.	D	15.	B	21.	D
4.	C	10.	C	16.	B	22.	D
5.	C	11.	C	17.	A	23.	A
6.	A	12.	D	18.	C	24.	D
						25.	C

Test 8

1.	C	7.	A	13.	B	19.	D
2.	D	8.	B	14.	A	20.	C
3.	D	9.	A	15.	A	21.	B
4.	C	10.	C	16.	B	22.	C
5.	A	11.	A	17.	D	23.	A
6.	B	12.	D	18.	D	24.	A
						25.	A

Test 9

1.	C	7.	B	13.	B	19.	A
2.	A	8.	A	14.	A	20.	B
3.	B	9.	A	15.	D	21.	D
4.	B	10.	D	16.	C	22.	C
5.	C	11.	B	17.	C	23.	B
6.	D	12.	D	18.	C	24.	A
						25.	A

Test 10

1.	A	7.	A	13.	D	19.	A
2.	D	8.	C	14.	C	20.	C
3.	A	9.	A	15.	B	21.	D
4.	A	10.	B	16.	B	22.	D
5.	C	11.	B	17.	B	23.	A
6.	B	12.	C	18.	C	24.	A
						25.	C

References

Anagramsite.com www.anagramsite.com/cgi-bin/getanagram.cgi names the bank www.rockroses.au, which is an anagram of 'www.crooks are us' Accessed 3 September 2009

Casciani, D (2008) *Analysis: UK gun crime figures.* BBC News http://news.bbc.co.uk/1/hi/uk/6960431. stm Accessed 4 September 2009

Connected (2009) http://connected.homeoffice.gov.uk/ Accessed 5 September 2009

Connected (2006) *The second Connected conference: Building on our work together to tackle guns, knives and gang-related crime in England and Wales* http://connected.homeoffice.gov.uk/assets/ docs/final_report_connected_two_conference.pdf Accessed 5 September 2009

Crimestoppers (2008) *One in ten young people affected by guns and knives* www.crimestoppers-uk.org/media-centre/crime-in-the-news/april-2008—crime-in-the-news/one-in-ten-young-people-affected-by-guns-and-knives Accessed 5 September 2009

Department for Transport (2009) *Reported road casualties in Great Britain: Quarterly provisional estimates* Q1 2009 www.dft.gov.uk/pgr/statistics/datatablespublications/accidents/rcgbQ12.009 Accessed 4 September 2009

Department for Transport (2004) *Tackling crime on public transport.* www.dft.gov.uk/pgr/crime/ tacklingcrimeonpublictransport Accessed 4 September 2009

Department for Transport (2006) Case study *New York City: A focused approach to rapid cleaning and removal* www.dft.gov.uk/pgr/crime/reducinggraffiti/casestudyreportongraffiti?page=3#a1002 Accessed 4 September 2009

Department for Transport (2004) *The school run. A training programme for bus drivers focusing on conflict resolution with school pupils* www.dft.gov.uk/pgr/crime/srtp/choolruntrainingprogramme 3007.pdf Accessed 4 September 2009

Department for Transport (2007) *Research on the personal security issues for taxi and PHV drivers – Executive summary* www.dft.gov.uk/pgr/crime/taxiphv/research Accessed 4 September 2009

Harlow Tennis Club *Constitution* (2009) www.harlowtennisclub.org.uk/constitution.htm Accessed 3 September 2009

Home Office (2009) *Crime and victims, Gun crime.* www.homeoffice.gov.uk/crime-victims/reducing-crime/gun-crime/ Accessed 4 September 2009

Malthouse, R and Roffey-Barentsen, J (2009) *Written exercises for the police recruit assessment process.* Exeter: Learning Matters

NPIA (2008) *Learning the lessons* Bulletin 4 www.learningthelessons.org.uk/learningthelessons june2008b.pdf Accessed 9 September 2009

NPIA (2008) *Learning the lessons* Bulletin 5 www.learningthelessons.org.uk/learningthelessons_bulletin_oct08_v4.pdf Accessed 9 September 2009

NPIA (2009) *Learning the lessons* Bulletin 6 www.learningthelessons.org.uk/learningthelessons_bulletin_feb09.pdf Accessed 9 September 2009

NPIA (2009) *Learning the lessons* Bulletin 7 www.learningthelessons.org.uk/learningthelessons bulletin_june09_web.pdf Accessed 9 September 2009

Places of Worship (2009) http://pow.reonline.org.uk/ Accessed 4 September 2009

Roffey-Barentsen, J and Malthouse, R (2009) *Reflective practice in the lifelong learning sector*. Exeter: Learning Matters

Sky News (2009) *Man jailed over 'parking rage' attack* http://news.sky.com Accessed 4 September 2009

Midgley, C (2007) Crystal meth: coming to a town near you. *Times Online* www.timesonline.co.uk/tol/life_and_style/health/article1755178.ece Accessed 4 September 2009

Ford, R. (2007) The facts of Britain's gun culture. *Times Online* www.timesonline.co.uk/tol/news/uk/crime/article1391199.ece Accessed 4 September 2009

What is Korfball? www.korfball.co.uk/whatiskorfball/whatiskorfball.html Accessed 3 September 2009

Index